Hiking in North Florida with William Bartram

25 Hikes

Volume Two

Also by G. Kent

Nonfiction

*Hiking in North Florida with William Bartram:
25 Hikes – Volume One*

*Running with Razors and Soul:
A Handbook for Competitive Runners*

Fiction

Bandits on the Rim

Grinners

Granada Hills Blood

Hiking in North Florida with William Bartram

25 Hikes

Volume Two

G. Kent

Bandit Press

© Copyright 2015 by Gary R. Kent

All rights reserved. No part of this book may be used or reproduced by any means, graphic, electronic or mechanical, including photocopying, recording, taping or by any information storage retrieval system without the written permission of the publisher except in the case of brief quotations embodied in critical articles or reviews.

ISBN-13: 978-0692493953
ISBN-10: 0692493956
LCCN: 2014-916980

Bandit Press
2329 NE 8th Place
Ocala, Fl 34470
kentib@earthlink.net

This book may be ordered from the publisher, through booksellers at Barnes and Noble, or online at createspace.com or amazon.com.

CONTENTS

Dedication	viii
Foreword by Todd Carstenn	xi
Introduction	1
Prologue – Hiking With Adults	4
Seasons	6
Wildlife and Insects	8
What To Carry	11
Rain and Lightning	13
Uphill and Downhill	15
Hunting	16
Firearms	18
Lost	20
Rangers	22
Leave It Alone	24
"Renascence" by Edna St. Vincent Millay	25

Hike # 1 – Goethe State Forest – Black Prong Trail	26
Hike # 2 – Goethe State Forest – Giant Cypress Trail	32
Hike # 3 – Ochlockonee State Park – Pine Flatwoods Nature Trail	36
Hike # 4 – Salt Springs Recreation Area – Bear Swamp Trail	39
Hike # 5 – Florida Trail – Big Shoals	42
Hike # 6 – Davenport Landing Trail	46
Hike # 7 – O' Leno State Park – Parener's Branch Trail	51
Hike # 8 – Gold Head Branch State Park – Florida Trail, Ridge Trail, Fern Trail and Loblolly Loop	55
Hike # 9 – Salt Springs Connector Trail	60
Hike # 10 – Silver Glen Springs Recreation Area – Lake George Trail	64
Hike # 11 – Florida Trail – Hopkins Prairie	68
Hike # 12 – Florida Trail – Woody's Trail North	72
Hike # 13 – Longleaf Flatwoods Trail	77

Hike # 14 – Florida Trail – Hidden Pond	82
Hike # 15 – Alexander Springs Recreation Area – Timucuan Trail	87
Hike # 16 – Billies Bay Wilderness	91
Hike # 17 – Florida Trail – Farles Prairie	94
Hike # 18 – Clearwater Lake Trail and Florida Trail from SR 42	99
Hike # 19 – Emeralda Marsh Conservation Area	103
Hike # 20 – Lake Norris Conservation Area	108
Hike # 21 – Guana River State Park	113
Hike # 22 – Fort King National Historic Landmark	117
Hike # 23 – Ross Prairie State Forest – Holly Hammock Trail	121
Hike # 24 – Carney Island Recreation Area	124
Hike # 25 – Withlacoochee State Forest – Oxbow and Johnson Pond Trails	128
Epilogue – We Have To Care	132
Happy Trails	133
"There Is Another Sky" by Emily Dickinson	134

Dedication

"One touch of nature makes the whole world kin."
                                        - William Shakespeare

"Nature is not a place to visit. It is home."
                                        - Gary Snyder

In 1773, a Philadelphia "city boy" named William Bartram embarked upon a four-year excursion to the Southeast American Colonies. By 1774 he reached what is known today as North Florida. The "Flowery Land" was, briefly, under British rule following their 1763 victory in the French and Indian War. Bartram explored and described the region at a time when there was virtually no European development. He also took notes and made drawings of much of the local flora and fauna. In 1791, Bartram's book *Travels* became an American classic, in large part because of his descriptions of a wild and untamed North Florida. Oddly, the book was read more in Europe than in the United States. In fact, many British romantic poets, including William Wordsworth and Samuel Taylor Coleridge, used imagery taken from Bartram's descriptions of North Florida in their poetry.

In Bartram's eyes, North Florida's spring-fed lakes, sandy shores and ancient forests formed a natural paradise. He wrote about the alligator as a "noisy dragon-like animal...with a horrifying roar." Modern biologists have confirmed Bartram's observations of group feeding and maternal care among alligators as accurate. The fragile celestial lily that he described and discovered near Lake Dexter off the St. Johns River was not found again for 150 years. Also, Bartram was the first to describe a Florida hurricane: "The furious storm sweeps along…and the face of the earth is obscured by the deluge descending from the firmament, and I am deafened by the din of thunder." I'm certain NBC weatherman Al Roker would confirm Bartram's description, especially after suffering from an infamous tumble at the hands of Hurricane Wilma in Naples, Florida while on the air in 2005.

During Bartram's journey, he visited several Seminole Indian villages. He strongly urged the U.S. Government to avoid warfare with the Florida Indians. He also suggested sending diplomats into Florida to learn the Seminole language and customs. Critics were skeptical of Bartram's sympathetic accounts of the Seminole, which challenged the popular presumptions that all Indians were inferior and primitive savages. Bartram's Quaker background and lifestyle, similar to William Penn's, compelled him to express the necessity of a humane public policy toward the Seminole and other major tribes. Unfortunately, Bartram's sensible advice was ignored, and three Seminole Indian Wars resulted.

The Florida State Parks motto is "The Real Florida." In 1774, William Bartram witnessed and experienced "The Real Florida" and the natural condition of its pristine environment. Our vision and quest should be to preserve and protect as much of "The Real Florida" as possible for the enjoyment of present-day and future generations. Although he lived and died in Philadelphia, North Floridians consider Bartram to be an honorary citizen of our state.

This book is dedicated to the vision and memory of William Bartram (1739-1823).

Foreword

"He stood breathing, and the more he breathed the land in, the more he was filled up with all the details of the land. He was not empty. There was more than enough to fill him. There would always be more than enough."
— Ray Bradbury

Why do we hike? I think we hike because each trip we take we shed unneeded clutter accumulated since the last time we took to the trail. The quote that precedes this Foreword, from Ray Bradbury's *Fahrenheit 451,* shows his character escaping an overly mechanized dystopia that has long since lost its way, its soul. This character, Guy Montague, retreats to a place we all love—the woods. THAT is where he "breathed the land in." So maybe it's those breaths, or the promise of them, that lead us out to the trail, or the bluff, the stream, the conservation area, to any of the fifty places Gary Kent describes for us in volumes one and two of *Hiking in North Florida with William Bartram.*

I can tell you why I hike and camp. I hike and camp because I'm not sure there is anything better for my soul than solitude. The sweet empty silence of solitude. I love my job. I get to discuss big-time literature with some really sharp kids. But there is no solitude in a classroom, or a boardroom, cubicle or office. Though I'm not anti-social, which this might suggest, it is what is NOT out there that is initially most appealing. Silence is different in the woods. A breeze through the pine trees at Pat's Island. Rain drops on those little ponds at Zay Prairie. The rustling of who knows what in a dense cluster of bushes. A sunrise songbird. These collectively are Nature's voice, her siren song. Maybe silence is not technically the right word, but it feels like silence in the deepest part of me, the part that only Nature reaches. The part that hiking leads me to.

So, we've talked about why he hike. But why do read hiking books? Because, if you have ever camped or hiked or wandered without the benefit of a car or truck fifty feet away, we're family. And we all like to hear tales of family. When I read Gary Kent's books, including his *Running With Razors and Soul*, but especially these two William Bartram hiking books, I often find myself smiling and nodding in agreement. It isn't just that he and I are old hiking buddies and I've been on more than a few of these trails, it's because hikers essentially all speak the same language. It is a specialized jargon formed from shared experiences of surprise bear meetings, leaky tents, chafed thighs, and badly marked trails. Yes, I smile and nod—we all do, because we've been there. Literally and metaphorically, we have been THERE.

Finally, we read hiking books because the descriptions therein are like pictures in a frame. No one

confuses the picture in the frame with the scene itself. But these word pictures, written by as much an artist as any master photographer, are invitations to experience that scene, frame excluded. THAT is why we read hiking books. In his book *Zen and the Art of Motorcycle Maintenance,* Robert Pirsig, discusses the frame relative to that mode of transportation. If you're not actually riding, "You're a passive observer and it is all moving by you boringly in a frame.
On a cycle the frame is gone. You're completely in contact with it all. You're *in* the scene, not just watching it anymore, and the sense of presence is overwhelming."

Have you ever been overwhelmed by what you've experienced while hiking? Are there moments (conjure them up right now, I'll wait…) that simply cannot be removed from your consciousness?

I thought so.

Gary's books encourage us to get outside the frame, to immerse ourselves in the scene itself. To not be a passive observer. His books then, the framed descriptions of the hikes he knows intimately, are simply invitations: Once more to the woods. Come on. Let's go.

Todd Carstenn
Ocala, Florida

Introduction

*"Everyone must believe in something...
I believe I'll go hiking."*
- Fis Robin

*"I cannot endure to waste anything so precious
as autumnal sunshine by staying in the house."*
- Nathaniel Hawthorne

I've suffered a bit of grief from friends and others by claiming in Volume One that North Florida is as beautiful as Utah. Actually, Utahns have been gracious. It's folks from Colorado and California who have made the most fuss.

Okay, I raise the white flag. Those states are gorgeous. I never said the western states weren't God's country. Also, I was born and raised in California, so I'm very familiar with its striking mountains, beaches and deserts.

The point is my adopted state is also stunningly gorgeous in a very unique way, especially when it's not too hot to enjoy it. I have hiked and backpacked all over America, and there's one thing I know for sure—North Florida has the finest winter hiking and backpacking in the nation. Try to enjoy those great Colorado trails when it's five degrees and the trailhead is buried under six feet of snow. In winter, the North Florida snakes and bugs are practically non-existent, and it's not the hurricane or rainy season. Our winter days, usually sunny with clear skies, average highs of 65 and lows of 45 degrees. It rarely gets below freezing. To Floridians, temperatures in the thirties seem like below zero. It can get cold in North Florida, but not Fargo cold. Robert Byrne wrote, "Winter is Nature's way of saying 'Up yours'." Not in North Florida. In winter you can experience outdoor pleasures such as hiking, kayaking, mountain biking, backpacking, horseback riding and fishing, wearing little more than jeans and a long-sleeved shirt. I've always believed the Ocala National Forest should be proclaimed the National Mecca for winter hiking and backpacking.

    North Floridians are also accustomed to the good-natured ribbing about our highest mountain being 300 feet. Good one, I say, I never heard that before. The nearest beach to Denver is 1,500 miles. But North Florida is so much more than pretty beaches, and we get little or no press other than the Daytona 500 and Disneyworld. North Florida has crystal-clear springs, rivers and lakes, primordial sub-tropical prairies and swamps, and vast swaths of longleaf, loblolly and sand pine wildernesses. Few natural habitats are more impressive than a North Florida oak hammock.

    In Volume One of *Hiking in North Florida with William Bartram,* I presented 25 of my favorite hikes in this region that I have called home for the past 40 years. Volume Two picks right up where the first left off, with 25 more hikes in places that Mother Nature has blessed. The hikes are mostly two to four miles in length and should be walked at a leisurely pace in order to be experienced and enjoyed. After all, life is not always a workout.

There's the first trail up ahead. Lace up your hiking boots and load the daypack. North Florida is ready to sparkle.

Prologue – Hiking With Adults

"Wine is constant proof that God loves us and loves to see us happy."
                          - Ben Franklin

"I cook with wine, sometimes I even add it to the food."
                          - W. C. Fields

This hiking book is for adults, whether it be the guys, ladies, couples or soloists. Living the daily grind can be quite stressful. Adult life is both difficult and challenging, and the stress can cause an array of maladies, including anxiety, depression, headaches, stomachaches, and simple frustration. One great way to deal with these assorted ills is to get outdoors and enjoy the beauty and wonder of the natural world.

Unfortunately, the presence of children on a trail can hinder adult thought, adult conversation and adult activity. Some of those adult activities may include an adult beverage or a blanket for adult shenanigans.

You are not being a selfish or irresponsible parent for desiring a short period of down time away from the children. In fact, if adults are stressed out and frustrated with their lives, it can adversely affect their ability to raise the kids.

If you must have a child along, bring Bowser. He's a kid in a dog suit, and I guarantee he'll enjoy and appreciate the trail much more than the three-year old.

Adults require and deserve the right to decompress from their daily stressful lives. What better place to relax than on a North Florida hiking trail?

Seasons

"It was the earliest morning, when even the small trees cast long shadows, and scarlet foxes trot denward through the dew like flecks of fire."
— Gene Wolfe

My first morning in North Florida was in August 1974, and it was quite an eye-popping experience. At 8:30 a.m. the temperature was already a stifling ninety-three degrees and it felt like liquid heat, even in the shade. I took one sip of my hot coffee and tossed the remainder on the ground. Sultry? Yeah, I'll go with sultry. But that's like saying the Mojave is arid.

My mother-in-law's three-acre field was well manicured with scattered oaks and pine. After walking about fifty feet, I was sweating profusely, but I was still determined to explore the fence line. At least the grass felt good on my bare feet.

On my next stride, I kicked a stinging nettle and let out a yelp. When I bent over to rub my burning toes, three or four horseflies bit my left leg and I yelped again. As I attempted to escape the horseflies, I stepped on a fire ant mound. Fifty red ants simultaneously chomped on my right leg. I brushed off the ants and made a mad dash for the shade, yelping like a hyena.

Now I was drenched in sweat. On cue, a squadron of mosquitoes dive-bombed my face.

"I'll never survive here," I moaned.

By the end of the following summer, however, I was acclimated and felt like a native Floridian. I loved to go for a run in the summer with my non-Floridian friends and watch them wilt after the first mile.

Fall, winter and spring are awesome in North Florida, but we pay the price with a five-month May to September summer. The seasonal joke on Minnesota is that the state has two seasons, winter and July. We are not Minnesota's opposite. From October to April, it is very pleasant in North Florida. We have fewer bugs and snakes, less humidity and little rain. Hurricane season is over at the end of October. At times it can get cold, but for the most part, it's days of sweet cool air and sunny skies. Also, most tourists are visiting Universal Studios, Disneyworld and Daytona Beach. When the mountains in Yellowstone are buried under a blanket of snow, our fifty-five degree average temperature transforms North Florida into a Winter Wonderland. Just be sure to stay away in the summer.

I invite all hikers, backpackers, kayakers, mountain bikers and any other outdoor enthusiast to come to North Florida from October through April. Enjoy our trails, rivers, lakes and forests. See if you don't agree that North Florida is a Winter Wonderland.

Wildlife and Insects

"The frog philharmonic of the Florida lakes and marshes is unendurable in its sweetness. I have lain through a long moonlit night, with the scent of orange blossoms palpable as spilled perfume on the air, and listened to the murmur of minor chords until I thought my heart would break with the beauty of it."
- Marjorie Kinnan Rawlins

Florida's wildlife is exquisite. But please remember that the key word here is "wild". These animals are untamed and unpredictable. Even a squirrel may bite if you get too close. Of course, you could be safe and just leave them alone. North Florida bear, bobcat or alligator will not pick a fight, but they can all finish one. Be smart and give all wild animals their space. Observe and enjoy, but stay back. If confronted, always stand your ground and make noise.

In a remote area along the Ocklawaha River, my black Labrador Woody and I ran into a bobcat. He had beautiful markings, and I was rather surprised by his size. The average bobcat is 25-35 pounds, and this one appeared much larger. Woody, however, weighed 95 pounds, and when this elusive cat attempted to flee, my dog was right on his bobtail. I screamed for him to come back until I was hoarse. Suddenly the cat slowed down and made a few furtive glances at his pursuer. I feared a counterattack was imminent. To his credit, Woody sensed danger and gave up the chase.

"That little kitty could scratch your nose off, you big lummox," I said, "and much more."

What are people afraid of most? Snakes! Let me tell you, snakes are the biggest cowards and will do practically anything to get away from you, unless you mess with them. Even a little garter snake will bite if threatened. Some of the tougher ones, like moccasins and rattlesnakes, will coil and make a stand if teased or pursued. It's a last resort and you'd be wise to not take up the challenge.

Most North Florida bears are extremely wary of humans and will almost always attempt to avoid contact with them. Sadly, one exception may be "food-conditioned" bears. If people feed a bear, it can lead to dangerous situations for the human and the bear, especially the bear. "A fed bear is a dead bear," says naturalist John Hechtels. An aggressive bear could hurt someone, and if that happens he'll be a dead bear. I was shocked to find "Tygers" listed among North Florida wildlife in William Bartram's *Travels*, but a footnote explained native Floridians called panthers Tygers. Unfortunately, with the possible exception of a rogue, there are no more panthers in North Florida.

I humbly apologize for not being a bird expert, but I certainly enjoy and appreciate them. This month, I saw a bald eagle circling the parking lot at a Publix supermarket. At home I have several bird feeders and especially love to watch the cardinals. Male cardinals get all the press, because of their stunning red feathers, but I prefer the females. Female cardinals have more personality. They will look directly at you, cock their heads and chirp as if saying, "Get off your butt and go watch some other bird." Okay, I will. On the rivers, lakes, prairies and flatwoods, I'm sure that North Florida's 514 known bird species will amaze and entertain you as they do me.

A word about North Florida's bugs. Yep, we've got a horde of them. Last summer, I was working in my yard when I felt the prick of a flu shot on my right arm. I looked down and discovered a mosquito the size of a small bird greedily chugging down my blood. It appeared to have a dozen legs and antennae and looked like something from the barroom scene in the movie *Star Wars*. I swatted him with my left hand and a dollop of blood sprayed up my arm.

That's what we contend with in North Florida. Every other kind of stinging, biting and zapping pest lives here too.

Always carry bug spray, even when it's cold. Although the bug population is quite limited in the winter, you may still be ambushed by small surviving patrols. It's always a good idea to spray hiking boots, socks, and pant cuffs in order to discourage ticks, chiggers and brown recluse spiders. Personally, I like to use Skin-So-Soft because it's better for your skin and smells nice, but it's also oily and works only in short durations.

What to Carry

"Today something unusual happened. I was walking without even knowing where I was going. I got the power to love myself, nature and the rest of humankind. Cheers, everyone."
- Santosh Kalwar

Every hiking book has its special list of what to carry on a day hike. My list is ordinary and certainly not complete. One item I recommend that most books don't mention is a lightweight chair. Any aluminum frame or foldup contraption will work. This may sound burdensome, but when you're ready to relax on the trail a chair is sweet.

Also:

> Hat
> Sunglasses
> Sunscreen
> Bug Spray
> Raingear
> Flashlight
> Matches or Lighter
> Compass
> Snacks
> Water
> Book or Magazine
> Knife
> Extra T-Shirt

Extra Socks
Extra Fleece or Sweatshirt
Whistle or Cow Bells or something to make noise. (Good to scare off animals or if you get lost.)

The extra T-Shirt is for the sweat on the hike out. If it's cold, a wet T-Shirt can be miserable. Extra socks are in case you stumble into muck or water.

I won't discourage you from carrying a first aide kit. My thought on the subject, however, is that if I'm hurt and can't limp out of the woods for a mile or two, I guarantee a first aide kit won't help. The medical team will have to fly me out aboard a chopper.

Now for the secret stuff. A blanket or sheet is great for naps or…sex. Yes, I said sex. If the weather cooperates, sex in the wild can be magical. Also, bring along your favorite adult beverage. Whether it is beer, spirits or fine wine, an adult beverage on the trail can always help with decompression. You want it cold? There are excellent small collapsible coolers for sale, or try my little trick. Take a one-gallon zip lock bag and put in ice along with your beer or wine, or use the ice for mixed drinks. The bag may leak slightly, but it's well worth the effort.

Rain and Lightning

"The best thing one can do when it's raining is to let it rain."
        - Henry Wadsworth Longfellow

I like to hike in the rain. I usually won't start a trail if it's already raining, but if a downpour arrives while on the trail, I enjoy putting on the raingear and forging ahead. In North Florida, it rarely rains longer than twenty minutes.

Always bring the raingear.

Winter is not the rainy season, but there still may be an occasional thundershower. If you hike with those who scoff about the rain, when the first pitter-patter begins and you drop your pack to slip on the raingear, you'll look like a Kit Carson or Jeremiah Johnson.

In September 2014, the University of Florida cancelled its opening season football game versus Idaho because lightning strikes were in the area. If officials were willing to clear a stadium of teams, cheerleaders, band, auxiliary and 92,000 fans because lightning strikes were in the area, what does that tell you?

Take lightning seriously.

If you see lightning, count to ten. If thunder arrives before you reach five, seek shelter immediately. On the trail, that means a low depression, under a kiosk, deck or clump of small trees. Stay away from the tall boys because they act as lightning rods. Place your raingear on the ground to act as a conductor, and squat on the balls of your feet. Place your hands over your head and ears, and make yourself the smallest target possible. Wait it out and play it safe. Lightning can come suddenly and vanish quickly. Stay calm.

North Florida is part of a "lightning corridor" from Tampa to Jacksonville. In 2012, there were 901,381 flashes. Is North Florida the lightning capital of the world? Almost. I discovered that Rwanda in Africa has almost 2 ½ times the lightning strikes we have in North Florida. But we're # 2. Keep in mind, the greatest number of strikes occur during summer, when you won't be here.

Also, your chances of being struck are still near zilch. A flash followed by a crashing boom will scare the pants off the most courageous outdoorsman, but you have little to fear if you stay sensible. Respect the power of nature, wait out the storm, and then enjoy the rest of your hike.

Uphill and Downhill

"My soul can find no staircase to heaven unless it be through earth's loveliness."
- Michelangelo

"Of all the paths you take in life, make sure a few of them are dirt."
- John Muir

In Volume One, I wrote: "Uphill and downhill do not enter the equation in North Florida."

This has not changed. You want hills? Go to Rome, or San Francisco. The Sunshine State has some rolling terrain, but as a rule the trails are as flat as an IHOP pancake.

Enjoy.

Hunting

"I ask people why they have deer heads on their walls. They always say because it's a beautiful animal...I think my mom is attractive, but I have photographs of her."
- Ellen DeGeneres

"Hunters will tell you that a moose is a wily and ferocious forest creature. Nonsense! A moose is a cow drawn by a three-year old."
- Bill Bryson

Though not a hunter, I strongly support and defend hunting as a part of the American heritage, and those who practice it as legitimate sport. But I don't like hunters who use dogs or deer stands.

Do you know how bear hunting was conducted in North Florida when it was legal? A pack of dogs chased the bear up a tree, and the hunter would saunter up and shoot the helpless thing in the head. How is that sport? What part of that scenario is hunting? I'm also surprised the Humane Society isn't up in arms over the horrendous way many hunting dogs are housed and treated. Today, Florida is considering making bear hunting legal again. Plus, some unscrupulous hunters purposely send their dogs into wilderness areas, where hunting is illegal, in order for the dogs to flush out and chase the deer into areas where hunting is legal. Rangers at Alexander Springs Recreation Area have told me hunting dogs routinely run through the swimming area from Billies Bay Wilderness during hunting season. I've witnessed packs romp through the Juniper Prairie Wilderness. Besides being obviously illegal, this practice is cowardly.

I also don't like deer stands. Putting out a salt lick or corn niblets, and then waiting in a tree to shoot a clueless deer is not challenging nor does it constitute hunting. Look up the word "hunt" in the dictionary. Definitions will include words like search, seek, find, stalk, pursue and chase. Sitting in a deer stand is not hunting, it's waiting. If you're waiting, you're not hunting. Get off your ass and go hunt!

My biggest gripe with hunting is that the season takes up 2 ½ months of the prime-hiking period, usually from November 1st to mid-January. Geeesh! I suggest we extend the hunting season for an extra month or two, and in exchange we switch the months to June, July, August and September. That way, we leave October to March for the hikers. Too hot in the summer to hunt? C'mon, guys, hunters are tough. A little heat shouldn't bother them. Give the cool weather back to the tree-hugging hikers.

Firearms

"I'm glad I will not be young in a future without wilderness."
- Aldo Leopold

I must preface this rant by stating I am a gun owner and support the rights in the Second Amendment to the Constitution. I own two .38 revolvers, a .357 and 30-30 rifle. It's not much of a collection, but I do like the guns and enjoy shooting them. I don't, however, support guns on the trail. You certainly don't need a firearm for the animals: none of them will hurt or bother you unless you initiate a confrontation. That means you're bringing the firearm for people. Well, guess what? People hiking the trails are probably the most decent and law-abiding people in the land. Serial killers usually don't take a day off to hike a nature trail. In fact, a hiking trail is probably one of the safest places you can be in America.

I also don't want to be lumped into the group of gun owners who believe any attempt at gun control, no matter how sensible, is the first step toward a government conspiracy to take away and ban all guns. The NRA and unscrupulous politicians play on those fears to bolster gun manufacturers' profits and garner support and votes. What sane person really thinks gun registration, waiting periods and background checks are efforts by a secret government clique to seize all guns from the American citizenry?

Nor do U. S. citizens need automatic rifles or armor-piercing bullets. Who wants an unstable person to be able to wander into a gun show and stroll out with an AK-47? This type of lunacy invites more Columbines and Sandy Hooks. Now the NRA wants to allow students to carry guns on campus. Revoke the Second Amendment? Absolutely not! The President and Supreme Court do not have the power to revoke Amendments. Only State Legislatures can ratify or amend a Constitutional Amendment, and a majority of three-quarters of the states (38) is needed to do it. That's not going to happen to the Second Amendment.

In the 1930s, Nazi Germany began a systematic effort to seize all guns from its private citizenry. Well, the United States is not Nazi Germany and our President is not Adolf Hitler. Any news station or talking head attempting to make a comparison between the modern United States and 1930s Nazi Germany is not only being disingenuous and politically motivated, but also suffering from extreme right-wing paranoia.

Lost

"I love nature, I just don't want any of it on me."
- Woody Allen

"I've never been lost, but I was mighty turned around for three days once."
- Daniel Boone

You're hiking with a group, and then you stop for a pee break. "Go on," you say, "I'll catch up." Everyone needs a little privacy. It takes three minutes and you're on your way, but soon you reach a fork in the trail. You go left and hike fast for twenty minutes, but you don't catch up. You go right at another fork and hike for ten minutes. Nothing.

What to do?

Or you're hiking alone to a special point of interest. It's only two miles. You think you've followed the right trail, but you've hiked for forty-five minutes and know you should have reached your destination. You come to a junction and go right for another twenty minutes. Nothing. You think you're close to your spot, but suddenly feel confused and all turned around.

What to do?

First off, don't hike any further. Try to retrace your steps. If you think you are lost, DO NOT LEAVE THE TRAIL. Here are my nine steps to follow:

1. Breathe. Relax. Look around. Don't worry.
2. Take an inventory of your pack, just in case. Hopefully you'll find water, food, matches, knife, rain gear and a warm top. If you have that stuff, you'll be okay.
3. Make noise with your whistle or cowbell. Clap your hands. Yelling usually won't be heard and will give you a sore throat.
4. Look for landmarks and other people.
5. Never try a shortcut or leave the trail.
6. Don't run or panic. Don't quit mentally.
7. If you can start a fire, do so in a contained area. Smoke might be seen.
8. Forget the movies. Roving packs of animals or backwoods mutants will not murder you. Weather will be your biggest threat.
9. If you become exhausted, stop hiking. If you keep trying to hike, you'll get even more fatigued, frustrated and grumpy.

Chin up. Put on your game face. People are probably already looking for you. You will get out of this with a great story.

Rangers

"All nature wears a universal grin."
                              - Henry Fielding

    Friends tell me I possess a kind of smirk with an aura of mischievousness much like Woody Woodpecker. I can't help it. I have an attitude in the woods. Most rangers sense it and immediately become defensive.

    I like to bring a dog on the trail without a leash. I enjoy an adult beverage. I like to stay out after dark with a fire. I know there are many rules and regulations in our forests, and it's the rangers who must enforce them. Also, I know our parks are filled with many thoughtless pinheads, and it's the rangers who must deal with them.

    One reason I love wilderness areas is that they have fewer restrictions, and fewer people. Last year, my brother and I stood at a trailhead in Kings Canyon National Park in California. One trail went to Bubbs Creek and the other to Paradise Valley. The one to Bubbs Creek was closed due to flooding and roped off.

    I shook my head. "I really wanted to sit next to Bubbs Creek."

    My brother said, "It sure would be a great place to drink our wine."

A ranger marched up with a scowl and growled at us, "Don't even think about it, buster. The creek is swollen and you could drown if you try to cross it. You could also face a stiff fine."

"Dude, how can you fine me if I'm not there, or dead?"

"Don't sass me, son. I'll throw your ass out of the park."

"We were only talking about the trail," my brother interjected.

"No, you weren't," the ranger countered. "I saw the smirks on your faces. You were just waiting for me to leave before you slipped under the rope."

He may have had a point.

"Okay," I said, "you win."

I have met fine rangers. They are the front-line defenders of the American environment. They serve in the trenches of the environmental wars and deserve our respect. Without them, all would be lost. In fact, their jobs become increasingly difficult and stressful each year because funding is abysmal and federal and state governments don't seem to care. William Bartram would not be happy.

So, when rangers are around I do my best to be respectful and suppress my Woody Woodpecker attitude. Other times? Well, posted rules and trail signs are really just guidelines. I take responsibility for my decisions, and I am always respectful of the natural environment. That's the attitude that's most important to me.

Leave It Alone

"I like it when a flower or a little tuft of grass grows through a crack in the concrete. It's so fucking heroic."
- George Carlin

    Please do not deface or take any natural feature or historical artifact from any of our parks or preserves.
    Please do not litter. It's like a spit in the face to America.
    Kill nothing but time.
    Leave only footprints, take only photos and memories.

Renascence

And all at once the heavy night
Fell from my eyes and I could see, –
A drenched and dripping apple-tree,
A last long line of silver rain,
A sky grown clear and blue again.
And as I looked a quickening gust
Of wind blew up to me and thrust
Into my face a miracle
Of orchard-breath, and with the smell, –
I know not how such things can be! –
I breathed my soul back into me.
Ah! Up then from the ground sprang I
And hailed the earth with such a cry
As is not heard save from a man
Who has been dead, and lives again.
About the trees my arms I wound;
Like one gone mad I hugged the ground,
I raised my quivering arms on high;
I laughed and laughed into the sky.

Edna St. Vincent Millay

Hike # 1

Goethe State Forest Black Prong Trail

"Nature reflects the moods of a wizard."
- Deepak Chopra

*"From ghillies and ghosties,
and long-legged beasties,
and all things that go boomp in the night,
Good Lord, deliver us."*
- Old Scottish Prayer

Directions – From Dunnellon, drive 15 miles north on SR 41 to Morriston. Turn left (west) on CR 326. Go 6 miles to CR 337. Turn right (north). Black Prong trailhead is one mile north on the left (west) side of the road.

If you like the idea of being in the middle of nowhere, the Black Prong Trail is just for you. The trail is located in the remote Goethe State Forest west of Ocala. If you've never heard of the Goethe State Forest, join a very large club. The forest is also in the middle of nowhere.

The Goethe has 53,587 acres and was named after J. T. Goethe, from whom most of the land was purchased in 1992 under Florida's Conservation and

Recreation Land (CARL) program. The forest is managed for timber production, wildlife habitat, outdoor recreation and ecological restoration. Hunting is allowed in season.

Starting in the early 1900s, the acres in the Goethe were logged and turpentined. However, for fifty years prior to the state's purchase, during the time of Goethe's ownership, the land and trees were left virtually untouched. The forest contains many giant oaks and cypress, and some longleaf pine over 200 years old. The extensive old growth acres have one of the largest endangered red cockaded woodpecker populations in the state. Bear, white-tailed deer, Sherman's fox squirrel and wild turkey roam the woods, while bald eagle, hawk and turkey vulture patrol the skies. More than 100 bird species can be observed in their natural habitats. The Goethe State Forest also contains nineteen different natural communities, each with its own unique plants and animals.

Goethe has seven trailheads that offer hikers and horseback riders an unprecedented opportunity to explore an isolated wilderness that most Floridians don't even know exists.

The Black Prong Trailhead is open to hiking, backpacking and equestrian activity. On its several loops, it's possible to hike over fifteen miles. You can wander the tract for hours or hike out just a mile to get a taste. I suggest heading out from the trailhead and, after about 300 yards, turn left on the orange trail. Hike 1.5 miles, then turn right on the blue trail and work your way back to the parking lot for a total of about 3.5 miles.

This section of the Black Prong Trail offers a scrubby flatwoods that includes oak hammocks, occasional palm groves and towering longleaf pine. Though thick walls of vegetation block most of the views, when you do happen upon an open expanse it can be amazing. And the sky is often a deep blue with clouds that appear to billow and drip like a Salvador Dali painting. For a peek at what you'll experience on the hike, Google "Black Prong Trail" and click on "Hiking at Goethe State Forest (Black Prong Tract) YouTube" for an excellent 5:51 minute video from the trail.

One great reason to hike out here is the solitude. You are *way* off the beaten path in an area virtually undiscovered by most North Floridian hikers. True, you may have turned off a paved road to reach the parking lot, but it is a paved road *way* off the beaten path. The spooky movie *Jeepers Creepers* (2000) was filmed on these roads because they *are* out in the middle of nowhere.

Also, there's Bigfoot. Over a dozen reports of the hairy beast have come out of the Goethe State Forest since 2007. Google "Bigfoot in the Goethe State Forest" and check out the stories and pictures. I do have one question. How come every one of these so-called photos of Bigfoot are blurred or distorted? Don't any of these Bigfoot aficionados have a decent camera? Okay, that's two questions.

On my most recent trip to the Black Prong Trail, I sat on my blanket in front of one of those rare expanses and prepared for what promised to be a spectacular sunset. The pop from my wine cork echoed in the air. Suddenly, a loud crashing noise propelled its way through the woods directly toward me. I leaped to my feet and braced for a deer, bear or band of Sasquatch. Instead, it was an odd-looking young fellow with spiked hair and thick glasses. I recognized James E. Lindsay – Bigfoot Researcher. He carried an impressive-looking leather briefcase.

We stared at one another.

"You!" he cried, after recovering from his initial shock. "What are *you* doing out here?"

"Hello, James," I said. "Care for a cup of wine?"

I had met James E. Lindsay earlier in the year at Ocklawaha Prairie north of Lake Weir. He had been investigating what was considered to be a reliable Bigfoot sighting on the prairie by a couple of retired schoolteachers.

I said, "You're not still mad at me for scoffing at the investigation, are you?"

"Nope," he said. "My interview with the teachers went well and I believe their claim is creditable." He took a sip of wine.

I grinned. "Are you doing an investigation in the Goethe?"

He looked up. "You've heard the stories?"

"A few."

"Two months ago, a hunter spotted some scrapings on a tree, higher than any native animal could make. He later claimed that something was 'flanking' him. It only moved when he moved. I found the tree less than a mile from here."

This time, I was careful not to make sport. James E. Lindsay was a serious young man and I had already hurt his feelings once.

"Is that what you're investigating?"

He shook his head. "I'm investigating something far more intriguing. A woman named Denise Deschenes claims she's seen Bigfoot and has unknowingly photographed it right here on the Black Prong Trail. She said, 'I heard them walking with me. I know they're here.' She constantly used the plural 'them', indicating she believes there's more than one."

"When did this happen?"

"A month or two ago. Deschenes still hikes out here and has developed an unusual ritual before her hikes that she believes draws the Bigfoot to her. Before entering the woods, she prays, waves, meditates and calls out 'Hello.' She also leaves gift baskets containing beef jerky, crackers and tobacco. The Bigfoot Field Researchers Organization (BFRO) says it's not unusual for Bigfoot to accept gifts from humans and that sometimes Bigfoot will leave gifts in return, like unusual rocks or nuts that aren't from the local area. Denise Deschenes claims Bigfoot has left her stick and plant arrangements."

When James mentioned beef jerky, I immediately thought about those silly commercials with a Bigfoot tossing juvenile pranksters into the air. I fought it hard, but couldn't stop myself from bursting out with laughter.

"Dude," I chortled, "that lady's story is so lame."

He frowned. "You'll never be a believer."

"Guess not," I said. "I'm sorry, James. Don't be mad."

"The woman's story was in the newspapers." He finished his wine and snapped shut his briefcase. "You put out too many negative vibes. I'm outta here."

Once again, it was getting dark and I was alone in a remote area with numerous recent Bigfoot sightings. The frogs and crickets began their cacophony.

Bigfoot, I thought. Yeah, right.

I corked my wine. "Hey, James," I yelled. "Wait up."

Hike # 2

Goethe State Forest Big Cypress Trail

"If you're not a tree hugger, then you're a what, a tree hater?"
- Doug Coupland

Directions – From Dunnellon, drive 12 miles north on SR 41. Turn left (west) on CR 464. Go 5 miles to SR 121. Turn left (southwest). Cross CR 331 and continue for 4 miles to Cow Creek Road (dirt). Turn right (north) and drive 4 miles to Big Cypress Trailhead on the left (west) side of the road.

The Big Cypress Trail is located in the heart of the Goethe State Forest. The trail leads to an incredible bald cypress called the Goethe Giant, a humongous cypress with a nine foot diameter and more than 907 years old. The tree is a must-see. It was probably saved from the lumberman's saw because of its giant gnarls, which would hinder board making. However, since several other notable cypresses are nearby, inaccessibility may have also played a role in their survival. The Goethe Giant is the ninth largest cypress in the state, an impressive fact when considering the other eight are in the Corkscrew Swamp and Big Cypress Preserve in South Florida.

The Big Cypress Trailhead is located in the Cow Creek tract of Goethe State Forest. The four-mile drive on a safe but tiny dirt road will enhance the feeling of being secluded in the woods. The moment you start the trail you will be immersed in a primordial forest where rays of sun are rare. The trail is a one-mile roundtrip hike. You'll wander through flatwoods and hydril hammocks. Careful, the trail may be wet, but push on because it's well worth having muddy boots. Along the trail, you'll also encounter large oaks, magnolias and ancient loblolly pines. The Goethe State Forest is home to thirty-one different orchids, many which can be spotted from this trail or even on the dirt road.

Finally, the trail reaches a boardwalk that carries you above the basin swamp community to the Goethe Giant. You'll be out of the muck. Don't bother cleaning your hiking boots until you get back to the car. At the end of the boardwalk, linger and enjoy. Count the number of other large trees in the area. Use bug spray.

In William Bartram's 1791 *Travels*, he was the first to describe the beautiful and slinky red wolf, which once roamed the Goethe State Forest and was the top predator throughout the Southeastern United States. Unfortunately, the red wolf is currently extinct in Florida. By 1970, the entire population was less than 100. In 1980, it was officially declared extinct in the wild, and only 17 red wolves survived with 14 selected for a captive breeding program.

Today, the red wolf comeback is a huge success story, similar to the California condor comeback in the West. The Endangered Species Act of 1973 can work. In 1987, four breeding pairs of red wolf were released in the Alligator River National Wildlife Refuge (ARNWR) in Northeast North Carolina and by 1988 the first litter of pups was born in the wild. The Goethe State Forest in North Florida would make an ideal refuge for three or four breeding pairs of red wolf. They would flourish in the swampy areas of the Goethe, which are sparsely populated and similar to the ARNRW. The forest stretches all the way to the Gulf of Mexico.

Why do it? The major reasons are to prevent extinction and restore ecosystems where the red wolf once thrived. Also, because we owe it to the wolf. Human activity is the number one cause of the red wolf's demise. It's also the law. The Endangered Species Act of 1973 requires recovery efforts for federally listed endangered species. The presence of the red wolf in the Goethe State Forest would increase a balance to the ecosystem and significantly contribute to local economies by generating eco-tourist dollars. Conjure up a vision of standing by the Goethe Giant and spotting a red-eared buff colored wolf splashing among the big trees.

Red wolves are smaller than gray wolves, but larger than coyotes. Their average weight is 55 pounds and, according to a study of 2,206 scat samples collected by biologists in the Alligator River area in

2006, their diet is 100% deer, raccoon and small rodents. They don't attack cattle, which are too big, and there has never been a documented case of a red wolf attacking a human in 500 years of co-existence.

Imagine the howl of the red wolf in the Goethe State Forest.

Hike # 3

Ochlockonee State Park
Pine Flatwoods Nature Trail

"The earth has music for those who listen."
- George Santayana

"The lack of power to make joy in outdoor nature is as real a misfortune as the lack of power to take joy in books."
- Theodore Roosevelt

Directions – Ochlockonee State Park is 4 miles south of Sopchoppy on US 319.

Ochlockonee State Park is located on a scenic point where the Dead and Ochlockonee Rivers converge before emptying into the Gulf of Mexico. Several pre-Columbian Native American middens, or shell and refuse piles, sit on the shoreline of the Ochlockonee River. They were discovered in 1998 and date back 1,500 years ago. The area is in desperate need of a thorough archaeological dig.

    The Pine Flatwoods Nature Trail is an easy and pleasant 4.2 miles hike through a thick longleaf pine forest with cool breezes coming in off the two rivers and the Gulf. When the wiregrass is in bloom it creates a soft haze across the forest floor that is surreal and haunting. A large population of white squirrels adds to the eeriness. The squirrels are not albinos, but instead a genetic mutation of the gray squirrel, and their coats are snow white.

You also have a good chance of seeing the red cockaded woodpecker. Ochlockonee State Park is one of a few areas, like Goethe State Forest, that has a resident population of this endangered bird. They only nest in old-growth trees. Longleaf pines that are banded on the trail mark the nests of the woodpeckers. If you pause at the base of one of the trees, you'll probably see the candle-wax effect of sap spilling down the trunk, which was made by the woodpeckers to ward off snakes.

If you hike in the morning, every direction you face has a grayish haze, indicating marshlands or wet prairies. Look closely and you might see the rising sun glisten off the waters and pine needles. Eventually, you'll come to a boardwalk leading to an observation deck on Reflection Pond. Watch for turtles and alligators.

Ochlockonee State Park has a long-established prescribed fire program that mimics natural occurring wildfires. Since North Florida receives more lightning strikes than nearly any other place in the world, much of the animal and plant life is either fire dependent or fire adapted. By mimicking natural fires, park staff maintains an environment similar to the landscape of hundreds of years ago, and help to prevent dangerous and catastrophic wildfires such as the 1988 disaster in Yellowstone National Park. After uncontrolled blazes burned two-fifths of the national park, officials were forced to rethink the policy of immediately snuffing out natural wildfires. It was decided that prescribed burns, which eliminate large amounts of combustible material, can help prevent some of the devastating fires that have plagued the American West.

Similarly, Ochlockonee State Park's prescribed fire program has been effective and beneficial. It is an excellent model for forest management and care.

Hike # 4

Salt Springs Recreation Area Bear Swamp Trail

"There's a sunrise and sunset every day, and they're absolutely free. Don't miss so many of them."

- Jo Walton

Directions – Drive 0.2 miles north on SR 19 out of Salt Springs. Turn right (east) into recreation area. Sorry, it's a fee area. Turn left and follow the road into the campground. Turn right on the first one-way lane and follow it around to the overflow parking lot. Trailhead and sign are next to an old building.

Salt Springs Recreation Area is one of the jewels of the Ocala National Forest. The springs and camping areas are located in a lush, semi-tropical setting. The water is gin-colored and is fabulous for swimming and snorkeling. The presence of potassium, magnesium and sodium salts gives it a slight salinity, hence the name Salt Springs. In the early 1900s, many people came to Salt Springs believing it had medicinal healing powers.

Bear Swamp Trail is a 1.5-mile loop through an impressive old-growth forest and primordial swamp.

The trail runs parallel to Salt Springs Run, or River. Since the trail is located in a fee area, most hikers either don't know about it or ignore it. Most of the folks who pay the fee are coming to camp or enjoy a day of swimming in the springs. Also, it appears most of the campers lack the interest or initiative to go on the trail. That means this hidden gem can be considered one of our secret trails. The trail is not even listed in the park's brochure or on its website.

Bear Swamp Trail provides a glimpse into the type of ancient forest that undoubtedly hugged the shoreline of Salt Springs and its run at the time William Bartram visited the "amazing crystal fountain" in 1774. Many of these same trees provided shade for Bartram and his party. You can easily spend an entire afternoon on the trail. Since the loop is only 1.5 miles, when you finish, turn around and hike it again. I guarantee you'll see new things. The trail has a "Great Florida Birding Trail" designation. Also, on one of my visits, the ranger on duty claimed to have discovered 23 fresh bear tracks near the trail that morning.

The moment you enter the trail you'll be among massive Southern magnolias, dogwood, elm and several kinds of oak. The area is a perfect example of a big scrub hardwoods habitat. At the loop junction, turn in any direction and follow the yellow markers. It's unbelievable how quickly you become immersed in what feels like a movie set for one of the *Jurassic Park* or *King Kong* movies, while only 400 feet north is an RV campground.

Bear Swamp Trail is nicknamed "Oasis of the Ancients" for good reason. At 0.4 miles you'll pass through a large grove of loblolly pines, many of them quite tall and thick. When you start to notice the infusion of palm and cypress trees, you'll know the swamp is nearby. At 0.6 miles, a boardwalk appears, inviting you into Bear Swamp. Immediately, a dense tree cover that allows little or no sunshine and only a kiss of rain swallows you. The ground cover of the riverine swamp becomes wet.

Look on your right for a giant cypress. Reach over the railing and touch it. The trunk is eight feet around. The top is missing, a victim to either lightning or a hurricane. The large bumps on its trunk are probably what saved it from loggers. As you continue hiking on the boardwalk, several more large cypresses appear in the swamp, a few actually bigger than the first. The first branch of one of the cypresses is larger than any of the other tree species in the swamp.

When the boardwalk ends, continue your hike through a swath of huge palmettos that surround magnolias and loblolly pines. The crooked arms of rusty lyonia reach out to touch you. Look for the large resurrection fern atop a snag on the left.

At 1.5 miles you'll be back at the kiosk. Turn right and return to the parking lot…oh, no you don't. Turn around and hike the trail the other way.

Warning: beware of the crabby campground host. He may not be thrilled about your choice of parking. You paid the entrance fee—ignore him.

Hike # 5

Florida National Scenic Trail
Big Shoals

"It's as if I always met in those places some grand, serene, immortal, infinitely encouraging though invisible, companion, and walked with him."

— Henry David Thoreau

Directions – From Gainesville, take US 441 north through High Springs and Lake City. 5.3 miles north of Lake City, turn right (east) on Lassie Black Road. At 1.8 miles turn left (north) onto Morrell Drive. Follow road to the end of the cul-de-sac and continue through gate on a dirt road to the parking lot.

The 2.8 miles roundtrip Big Shoals Trail could quite possibly be the most varied and scenic trail in North Florida. It also takes you right up to the banks of the Suwannee River. Start your hike at the historic sign that introduces the Bishop family and their efforts to preserve the areas around the Big Shoals. You will march through a mature hardwood forest with plenty of ancient oak and loblolly pines.

Ticks can be a serious problem around the palmettos, so be sure to use bug spray on shoes, socks and pants. Also, spray around your waist. Watch out for poison ivy. This trail is rugged by Florida standards and is similar to many parts of the Appalachian Trail. There are inclines, roots, slippery rocks, and many places along the trail are overgrown with brush. Take care while hiking.

The trail immediately follows Bell Springs Creek with a crossing on a sturdy bridge. Bell Springs is a fourth magnitude (meaning small) spring that spews out 350 gallons per minute. After crossing the bridge, you'll begin to see the Suwannee River. After another crossing on wood beams, you'll be at the river's edge. Sandy banks invite you to view the river up close and personal. When I was there on 12-30-14, the river's water was brown with tannic acid. It's not dirty water. Rain washes tannic acid from trees, especially oak, into the river and causes the brownish tea coloring. During other months of the year, the water should be clear.

Next stop is Robinson Branch. You'll hear the branch and its falls long before you see it. At 1.1 miles you'll reach the falls. Falls? It's only about a four-foot drop, impressive for a Florida creek, but hardly a waterfall. For such a little tumble, however, it makes quite a racket.

Next, you'll reach another crossing. Trail guides claim this crossing is an easy ford. Yeah, right. A rope stretches across the branch so you can hold onto it while you wade across. On that same December day, the water temperature was 46 degrees and the dark water was waist high and higher. Even if you took off your hiking boots and stripped off your pants, your underwear would be sopping for the remainder of the hike. The cheap thrill would not be worth the inconvenience. I suggest bushwhacking thirty yards up creek and crossing over on a medium-sized downed oak that serves as a bridge. Don't try to cross it standing up unless you don't mind risking a plunge. This is another one of those "Here, hold my beer" moments. Since I am very balance-challenged, I crawled across to be safe. Once across, hike down the branch back to the river.

The first long-range view of the shoals is dazzling. As you climb a small knoll, watch for two spooky-looking oaks. At the top of the rise you'll have your view. The Big Shoals and surrounding area look like the wilds of Virginia or New Hampshire. Few Floridians would believe this is North Florida. Big Shoals is also Florida's only Class III rapids. The observation deck on the other side of the river is proof positive that it is nearly impossible to reach the river's edge from the State Park. Not so on the south side of the river. From the primitive campground, step down to the shoreline and find a comfortable rock. The sound from the shoals is almost annoyingly loud.

Pictures of Big Shoals on the Florida Hikes website do not do justice to this amazing destination. I can't accurately describe its beauty either, but I'll try to be eloquent. This place is cool! It's a keeper!

Hike back to the parking lot the same way you came.

Many people know about the Suwannee River from the famous song, which is actually called "Old Folks at Home." It's a minstrel song, written by Stephen Foster in 1851, and its lyrics are from the pre-Civil War years. It's also the Florida State Song. Ugh!

Stephen Foster was from Pennsylvania and had never been to Florida or seen the Suwannee River. He wasn't even writing about Florida or the Suwannee River. He needed the name of a river to fit the melody in the opening line. After rejecting the Yazoo River in Mississippi and the Pee Dee River in South Carolina, Foster settled on the Suwannee, but misspelled it 'Swanee' to fit the lyrics.

Unfortunately, there's controversy because the song offends a large segment of Florida's population. It uses ethnic slurs such as "darkeys" and is written from the perspective of a slave who is "longing for de old plantation." I don't believe most Floridians want our state to be associated with racism. Since the song is sung at the Governor's Inauguration, word changes have taken place in 1978 and 2003. Words may change, but the song's link to slavery has long been established.

It's time to dump the song. Please don't speak to me about heritage. Much of the heritage of the Old South is about slavery. Do we really need our State Song to bring up the subject? The song won't disappear. It's a catchy tune and might even become more popular from the attention. But there's no need for our state to be saddled with a song with such connotations.

Hike # 6

Davenport Landing Trail

"The best remedy for those who are afraid, lonely or unhappy is to go outside, somewhere where they can be quite alone with the heavens, nature and God."

- Anne Frank

Directions – Drive 9.5 miles north from Salt Springs on SR 19. Turn left (west) onto FR 74. Drive 2.5 miles west. Trailhead is on the right, just past the junction with FR 21. A sign will say Davenport Historical Site. Turn right and park next to the yellow gate.

Davenport Landing Trail is a pleasant 0.8-mile loop that takes the hiker to a historic landing on the Ocklawaha River. It is perhaps the most remote interpretive trail in the Ocala National Forest. The trail starts at the yellow gate. The first section of the loop is a tight fit among the foliage, and in desperate need of trail maintenance. If you prefer not to push through brush, go to the right at the loop junction and return the same way. If, however, you still want to hike the entire loop, turn left at the junction.

Watch for blueberry bushes on both sides of the trail. If the blueberries are ripe, keep a lookout for bear. Mulberry, saw palmetto and longleaf pines make up the forest. Also, scrub oak and the crooked arms of rusty lyonia. Soon the trail starts its descent to the river and its two kiosks. Steps lead to the river's edge.

The Ocklawaha River flows north into the St. Johns, which eventually flows through Jacksonville to the Atlantic Ocean. Its headwaters are the Green Swamp just north of Tampa and a large chain of lakes. Though heavily screwed up by the Army Corps of Engineers in their moronic efforts to construct the Cross Florida Barge Canal, its wild nature persists on a lonely thirty-mile stretch from SR 40 to SR 19.

In the late 1800s, Davenport Landing was the final high bluff that steamships would pass on their way up river from Jacksonville to Silver Springs. The landing was the last chance to pick up supplies and wood for the steam engines. The original landing master, Thomas Cassidy Fillyaw, a former Confederate soldier, is buried near the site.

This gorgeous river and its jungle-like forests attracted tourists who piled aboard specially built, tall and narrow, steamships that could navigate the slender river and its many twists and turns. Their final destination was an upscale hotel at Silver Springs, the largest springs in Florida. The Hart Steamship Line brought supplies and settlers to the rural communities along the river, as well as wealthy tourists to Silver Springs. The boats also brought out raw goods, such as turpentine, and pulled floating logs to the sawmills. Hart decked out several ships with luxurious accommodations for the tourists. Harriet Beecher

Stowe, of *Uncle Tom's Cabin* fame, made the journey and called the wild and scenic voyage "a visit to fairyland."

The two kiosks tell about the Hart Steamship Line and the Davenport Mound, an ancient Native American burial site first excavated by Charles Bloomfield Moore in 1894. The mound is the fenced-off area behind the kiosk. Though most of the artifacts have been looted, pieces of human remains at least 1,200 years old still rest within. Arrowheads found along the Ocklawaha River indicate human settlements as early as 10,000 BCE. Laws as well as human decency strictly forbid vandalizing or looting of the mound. Ancient burial mounds are just as sacred to Native American communities as modern cemeteries are to contemporary peoples and their societies. The Davenport Mound has a pinkish hue. Red ocher, a deep red iron ore, was ground and sprinkled into the sand over the dead. It was a common practice among Southeastern pre-historic Native American tribes.

From the two kiosks, hike down to the river in order to enjoy an incredible view both ways. The original stonework of the landing remains. Hopefully, you brought a chair or blanket. Davenport Landing is the most beautiful spot that can be accessed by hikers on the Ocklawaha River. The shoreline is an outstanding area for picnics and other activities. Stand at the river's edge. Chances are it will be only you and the river.

Unfortunately, our enchanting and beloved Ocklawaha River is still crippled and suffering. Dredging, changes to its course, and various locks and dams prevent the river from total recovery. Though work on the canal was halted in 1971, and the federal land was deauthorized in 1991 and turned into the Marjorie Harris Carr Greenway, much work remains in order to return the Ocklawaha River to its former glory.

Ms. Carr, a Florida environmental activist legend, always believed saving the Ocklawaha would be the greatest result from halting construction on the canal. However, a fierce debate over the fate of Rodman Dam and Reservoir, built as part of the canal's infrastructure, has erupted in North Florida. The dam and reservoir remain intact, and prevent the river from flowing freely. Just about everyone in Florida, including past governors and the majority of legislators, favor dismantling the dam and restoring the river. We ruined it; we need to fix it. The Florida Department of Environmental Protection has fought and won the legal right to draw down the reservoir and restore the river.

It's practically a done deal, except that a powerful group of elite fishermen and pro-development interests, including a handful of self-and-crony-serving congressmen, have worked tenaciously to block the dismantling of the dam. Ironically, officials have said that restoring the river would improve the fishing and local economy, and bring back the hardwood forests that once lined the river's edge. Bass, as well as manatee, would be able to swim freely up and down the river. Silver Springs and its river would also benefit.

It's time to stop this nonsense and waste of money, dismantle the idiotic obscenity and restore the Ocklawaha River. It's a good move for Florida and most of its citizens favor the idea. Since when do Florida legislators work for special interest groups who do not have the best interests of Florida in mind?

I know…trick question.

Hike # 7

O' Leno State Park
Parener's Branch Trail

To sit in the shade on a fine day and look upon verdure is the most perfect refreshment."
                                                - Jane Austen

Directions – Drive 6 miles north of High Springs on US 41. Entrance gate to O'Leno State Park is on the right (east) side of road.

The area around O' Leno State Park on the Santa Fe River north of High Springs has a fascinating history. There's also an incredible hike.

First of all, after flowing peacefully through the developed area of the state park, the Santa Fe River vanishes beneath the ground to become one of Florida's famous "disappearing rivers." It flows for three miles before re-surfacing at nearby River Rise Preserve State Park.

The natural three-mile land bridge over the river, created by sinkholes, was used as an important route and crossing point by generations of Native Americans, explorers and Floridians. Researchers believe Native Americans, including the Ocali and

Alachua, crossed the land bridge long before Spanish explorer Hernando De Soto camped nearby in 1539 on his way to the Georgia mountains and Mississippi River. Spanish missionaries traveling from St. Augustine to Pensacola used the bridge and even constructed the Mission de Santa Fe on the site. William Bartram camped along the river in 1774, and Seminole Indians roamed the area in the 1700s and 1800s.

It was the Santa Fe River and presence of the land bridge that led to the construction of the Bellamy Road in the 1830s (linking St. Augustine to Tallahassee), and the growth of a thriving little town known as Leno. Founded in 1840, Leno was originally called Keno after a popular bingo-like game played by gamblers. The town had a large casino and the usual social ills of a gambling town, such as brawls, gunfights and a red-light district. The law-abiding, church-going citizens of the town complained loudly when the town could not even attain an official post office with a name like Keno. City elders changed it to Leno.

At its height, just after the Civil War, Leno boasted two gristmills, a sawmill and six cotton gins, as well as the post office, general store, hotel, stables and a doctor's office. It thrived during the post-War Reconstruction. In 1894, Leno met its fate when the Santa Fe Railroad bypassed it in favor of Fort White to the south. Within two years, the town was a deserted ghost town. Well, not completely deserted. Notorious bands of thieves used the buildings in Leno as outlaw hideouts in order to assault travelers on the old Bellamy Road. After most travelers quit using the road, not only did the thieves depart, but it is said the ghosts pulled out too since there was no one left to scare. Leno then became known as Old Leno.

There is also a tale of a young Indian maiden, who was swimming with her lover in the Santa Fe, when she got sucked into the underground caverns where the river disappears. Whistling among the stones, caused by water suction, is believed to be her cries for help.

In 1935, Franklin Roosevelt's Civilian Conservation Corps arrived and built the core of what is now O' Leno (a form of Old Leno) State Park, one of Florida's first state parks. Perhaps the most remarkable achievement was the construction of a swinging suspension bridge that is still in use at the park today. Don't worry. The bridge is reputed to be able to carry an elephant.

Now for the hike.

O' Leno State Park is 6,000 acres of mostly old-growth forests. Parener's Branch Trail is a 3.69 miles loop that is perhaps the most stunning trail north of Gainesville. It meanders past several picturesque sinks, or ponds, lined by giant cypresses and with much of the surface water coated with green moss. Several benches offer a multitude of photo options. Take pictures of the ponds with the reflections of the huge trees. Count the many comical or evil faces among the cypress trunks.

This is truly a magical trail. The month of December, on a sunny day with temperatures in the 50s, is a perfect time to venture out and look for deer, bear and wild turkey. Hike the trail leisurely. You don't want to miss the many surprises that will greet you along the way.

By far, the most incredible feature of Parener's Branch Trail is the old-growth forest. Due to massive logging in Florida, it is difficult to discover trees that are as mature as the ones in O' Leno State Park. Do the math. The town came into in existence in 1840 and lay undisturbed after 1894. Many of these trees could easily be over 200 years old. The longleaf pines are some of the thickest and most towering in the state. Also, many of the oak and cypress are awesome. This forest is sumptuous and inspiring. I guarantee you'll not want to leave.

Near the end of the trail, O' Leno State Park offers a lesson for recovery from a southern bark beetle infestation. In 2001, several infested acres were cleared and burned. In 2003, longleaf pines were planted. Thirteen years later, many of these trees are 15 to 20 feet tall and suffer no symptoms of infestation.

After your hike, cruise into the town of High Springs for dinner at the splendid and historic Great Outdoor Café. If the weather cooperates, be sure to ask your pretty hostess for a table in the walled outdoor patio area.

Hike # 8

Gold Head Branch State Park – Florida Trail, Ridge Trail, Fern Trail and Loblolly Loop

"I felt my lungs inflate with the onrush of scenery – air, water, trees. I thought, 'This is what it is to be happy.'"
- Sylvia Plath

Directions – From Keystone Heights, drive 6 miles north on SR 21. Turn right (east) into the state park entrance. The Florida Trail trailhead is just inside the park entrance on the left (north) side of road. Parking is on the right (south).

Like O' Leno, Gold Head Branch State Park is one of Florida's four original state parks, developed on 2,300 acres by the CCC in the mid-1930s. The park is located on a patch of rolling sand hills known as the Central Ridge. A deep ravine bisects the area and forms the crystal clear waters of Gold Head Branch. The Branch was created by groundwater dripping off the steep sides of the ravine before emptying into Little Lake Johnson.

Deer, fox, gopher tortoise, coyote, Sherman fox squirrel and an array of raptors including bald eagle, red-tailed hawk, osprey and Southeastern kestrel roam the area. Also, there's a diversity of wildflowers and grasses such as blazing star, goldenrod and lopsided Indian grass.

Our hike is a combination of four trails, each with its own ecosystem. The sections of the Florida National Scenic Trail, Ridge and Fern Trail, and Loblolly Loop will add up for a total of 5.5 miles. The four trails will lead you through a variety of settings and hopefully keep you out of the way of most park visitors.

The 1.1-mile section the Florida Trail skirts the park's highest country and meanders through a mature forest of longleaf pine, blackjack and turkey oak. It also touches the southern edge of Deer Lake, where several spooky-looking rusty lyonia line the shore. Deer Lake is also known as Devil's Wash Basin, which begs the question, "What is going on around here?" I keep wondering why the state park is hiding the lake's original name. A coy female ranger at the entrance just giggled when I asked.

When the Florida Trail hooks up with the Ridge Trail, look for the Fern Trail immediately on your right. Take it and drop 0.4 miles to the bottom of the ravine. Note the striking changes in environment. In Florida, a change of 10-20 feet elevation can mean the difference between a dry pine flatwoods and a sub-tropical swamp. This ravine's ecosystem resembles the creek hollows of the Great Smoky Mountains National Park.

The fern-filled bowl features hickory, sweet gum and laurel oak.

At the bottom of the ravine is a wooden bridge and several other excellent observation points near Gold Head Branch, a small gin colored stream with an inviting white sand bottom. It is totally gorgeous. Take off your shoes and wade in either direction. It's only about a foot deep. The beautiful wood bridge is a perfect spot for rest and relaxation.

After you've taken your fill of the branch, hike back up the ravine and turn right on Ridge Trail. The trail hugs the upper lip of the ravine and provides many lovely views of its steep slopes. Hike for 0.9 miles to a second bridge over Gold Head Branch and to the site of an old mill. There's not much left of the mill except a small section of its foundation.

Re-cross the bridge and hike 0.95 miles on the Loblolly Loop. The Loblolly Loop Trail passes the largest loblolly pines in North Florida, many of them over 100 feet tall. Several benches invite you to relax and enjoy the expansive views of the forest. After finishing the loop, retrace your steps along the Ridge and Florida Trail to your car.

It's amazing how these four trails make you feel isolated inside a desolate wilderness—all within the boundaries of a popular state park. I saw one couple and one guy with his dog on my entire hike. As I approached the guy with the dog, I noticed that he appeared quite shaken and was in a big hurry. He informed me that he'd almost stepped on a huge eastern diamondback rattlesnake and his dog had actually jumped over it. I thought he was giving me a head's up.

"That'll get your heart pumping," I said.

"It was like a shot of adrenalin," he said. "I found a big log and crushed its skull."

I tilted my head. "You killed him?"

"Yep."

"Did he coil or rattle at you?"

"No," he said. "He just freaked me out."

I said, "Did he threaten you or your dog in any way?"

"Nope. He could barely move because of the cold."

I shook my head. "Then why'd you kill him?"

"He just freaked me out."

As I walked off, I thought, "You ignorant jackwagon."

Friends and fellow hikers, you're not supposed to go into a state or national park and kill the wildlife. It's not only illegal, it's immoral. I'd wager that snake would have moved off the trail by the time I reached the spot. You certainly shouldn't consider killing an animal that offers no threat to you or anyone else. This fear and loathing of snakes has got to stop. All snakes prefer to retreat when encountered, but can become defensive when threatened. Most snake bites occur when people attempt to kill, capture or pick one up. When left alone, snakes present no danger to anyone. They also play a crucial role in natural biodiversity and the food web. Please, do not kill snakes or any other creatures in the wild. You are a visitor in their home.

Hike # 9

Salt Springs Connector Trail

"For in the true nature of things, if we rightly consider, every green tree is far more glorious than if it were made of gold and silver."
                                          - Martin Luther

Directions – From Ocala, drive east on SR 40 for 28 miles. Turn left (north) on SR 19 and drive 9 miles. Just past the entrance to the Salt Springs River Trail on the right (east), keep a sharp lookout for several blue markers and a small Florida Trail sign on the left (west) side of road. It might take you more than one pass to find. If you enter Salt Springs, you've gone too far.

The Salt Springs Connector Trail connects the Florida National Scenic Trail to the tiny hamlet of Salt Springs. Do you know the purpose of a connector trail? It's supposed to be a trail that allows thru-hikers—those hiking a long distance trail from end to end— to leave the main trail for supplies. But this particular connector trail is a trail that absolutely no one uses. No thru-hiker is going to hike 5.4 miles roundtrip for a beer and Slim Jim when just six miles up the actual trail is the 88 Country Store, only 200 yards off the trail. Woo-Hoo! What we've got here is our very own secret trail with no hikers. And this trail is a beauty.

Park your car and follow the sky blue markers. The trail is well marked and maintained. A gorgeous Sabal palm greets you at the beginning of the trail with a noisy hawk on top that serves as a guardian. At .25 miles, the first of many large wet expanses with spring-fed ponds appears on both sides of the trail. Huge oaks blanket the rim on the right side, creating many great photo opportunities.

When I hiked this trail in mid-January 2015, the area was littered with a dozen or so Bud Light beer cans left by a company of thoughtless cretins. Are there really people who think natural areas look prettier with human trash strewn about, or do they just assume some tree-hugging geek like me will come along and tidy up their mess? Well, their plan worked to perfection this time. I crushed the cans with my boot and placed them at the bottom of my pack. It's always a commendable practice to leave a natural area nicer than you found it.

At 0.5 miles, you'll enter Riverside Island, an area of higher ground with a large forest of longleaf pine. Try to locate the oddly bent pine on the right side that starts out three feet high and then stretches forty feet horizontally before again turning skyward. This was a rare day on which no animals were sighted. On a better day, you should be able to spot deer, bear, fox, wild turkey and perhaps alligator in the wet areas.

At 2.7 miles the trail dead-ends at the Florida Trail. A sign and a sturdy bench mark the spot. The trail markers are now orange. At one time this was called the Ocala Trail, since it covered 67 miles of the Ocala National Forest. This was the first completed section of the 1300-mile Florida National Scenic Trail, and it seems the Ocala designation has been dropped so that the entire trail can be referred to as the Florida Trail. I don't like it. This section of trail should always be known as the Ocala Trail, a 67-mile segment of the Florida National Scenic Trail. But I digress.

I know you've covered 2.7 miles, which will be 5.4 miles after you get back to your car, but allow me to suggest a slight extension of your hike. Turn right (west) on the Florida Trail and continue for 1.5 miles. You will reach a grand and elegant section of the forest that I call the Little Valley. The spot was my focus destination for Woody's Trail in Volume One, and is an enchanting example of a rolling forest island. If you decide to hike to the Little Valley, your total mileage would be 8.4 miles, but it's well worth the effort. I met a Florida Trail volunteer at the junction and asked him if he had passed a wide depression loaded with longleaf pine. I didn't need to say anymore. His face lit up with recognition, and he said, "That place is awesome."

After you finish your hike, drive north for one mile on SR 19 and go for a quick dip at Salt Springs Recreation Area. The temperature of this first magnitude springs is a constant 72 degrees, and the snorkeling is an especially rewarding experience. Plus, in the winter months, Salt Springs plays host to a group of manatee trying to escape colder water temperatures.

West Indian manatees are magnificent and gentle creatures. In Florida, estimates have the manatee number at about 5,000 individuals. The manatee is Florida's State Marine Animal and can live up to sixty years. They are slow-moving and tolerant of swimmers, snorkelers and scuba divers attempting to pet them. However, they do have difficulty getting out of the way of speeding boats. After all, they're sea cows. Nearly every single manatee in Florida has at least one scar on his or her back from a boat propeller.

The main causes of death are human related issues such as habitat destruction and speeding boats. Although it would be nearly impossible to protect all the manatees from boats in all of Florida's waterways, during the winter months they do congregate near the heads of springs and other areas that have warmer water. Most of these areas have a "no wake, idle speed only" policy. That's nice, but HELLO! How about a "trolling motors only" policy? Canoes, kayaks and even electric trolling motors cause no harm to the manatee. All other watercraft needs to stay out of manatee habitat…period.

Hike # 10

Silver Glen Springs Recreation Area Lake George Trail

"Look! A trickle of water running through some dirt. I'd say our afternoon just got booked solid."
- Bill Watterson,
Calvin and Hobbes

Directions – From Ocala, drive 28 miles east on SR 40. Turn left (north) on SR 19. Go 6 miles. Entrance to Silver Glen Springs Recreation Area is on the right (east) side of road. Watch for sign.

Silver Glen Springs Recreation Area is a state and national treasure. Every day sixty-five million gallons of clear, clean and drinkable water shoot from its vents and pour into a run that empties into Lake George. Unfortunately, it's the popularity of Silver Glen Springs that may adversely impact its health and beauty.

Although most visitors access the park by land, many prefer to reach the springs by water. Littering and dumping, transporting hydrilla (which overwhelms native grasses) on boat propellers, improper placement of anchors, and climbing on the shorelines can cause irreparable damage.

As I gaze upon Silver Glen Springs or hike along its run to Lake George, I can't help but think about the numerous threats to our waters. Florida is surrounded on three sides by oceans and estuaries. The state averages billions of gallons of rainfall each year and is underlain by trillions of gallons of fresh groundwater in its aquifer. That's water in our lakes, rivers and springs, and water reflecting the sunshine along our endless estuaries and white sandy beaches. Water, clean and pure. No wonder we're known as the Water State.

We must do whatever it takes to keep it that way.

Most of Florida's waterways, including Silver Glen Springs, are threatened by irresponsible development and unregulated industries. Under the guise of economic growth and job creation, industrialized agriculture, mining operations, utilities, and fertilizer and chemical companies pollute, deplete and poison much of our water systems. This must come to a halt. Environmental groups need and deserve our support to wage war upon the greedy and unscrupulous scoundrels who despoil our state for monetary gain with little or no concern for the quality of life or, ironically, our economic appeal.

Okay, I'll stop.

After paying a $5.50 fee, walk down to the springs and stand at the water's edge. Look, and you will be amazed. If the day is in the high 60s or 70s, I suggest a quick swim following your hike. It will be exhilarating. On your left is an impressive midden, or Indian mound, with large oaks growing on top. Human beings have been drawn to Silver Glen Springs for thousands of years. Archaeological excavations have uncovered settlements dating back over 7,000 years. Please do not tread upon the midden. The Antiquities Act of 1979 protects the midden for the benefit of all Americans.

Walk through the picnic area and begin your hike to Lake George. This trail is a pleasant 2.3 miles roundtrip with a short loop off the lake. Once you start the trail, a sub-tropical palm and live oak hammock, draped with Spanish moss swaying in the wind, will immediately embrace you. You'll pass loblolly pines, several groves of Sabal palm, and clusters of magnolia and saw palmetto. Watch for deer amongst the thick woods, and osprey patrolling the skies above the water. Listen for their piercing cries.

At 0.8 miles you'll reach the beginning of the loop. A spur trail to the right leads to the first view of Lake George. There is a well-built bench to stand on for a better view. The lake is huge, six miles across and thirteen miles long, and is often covered with whitecaps.

Return to the fork and explore the loop. You will enjoy several more excellent views of the lake and the St. Johns River to the north. Hike along the split rail fence and look for wading birds such as blue heron, anhinga and sandhill crane. I most recently visited the Lake George Trail on December 8, 2014. It was a cold, windy and cloudy day. Other than the attendant's car, the parking lot was empty. In the summertime this lot and the overflow parking lot are usually full.

I hiked to the end of the spur trail and stood on the bench overlooking the lake. With its awesome whitecaps the lake resembled a small ocean. Spray from the lapping waves occasionally spritzed me in the face.

On my way back to the fork a Florida black bear stood in the middle of the trail nibbling on a bush. A bear on a short nature trail was the last thing I expected. Suddenly the trail closed in on me. Dark clouds formed a low ceiling and the path appeared to shrink before my eyes. My heart was pounding. I began to sweat. I tried to recall all my wise and calming advice about bear encounters. I only remembered to stand my ground. It's certainly a different game when confronting a bear by yourself.

Luckily, this was a good bear. He took one look at me and crashed into the palmettos with his butt in the air. As I hiked back to the springs, I took out my notebook and whacked it on my thigh to make noise. No need to run into Yogi again.

Hike # 11

Florida National Scenic Trail Hopkins Prairie

"The invisible world is a daily miracle, for those who have eyes and ears."
— Edith Wharton

Directions – From Ocala, drive 18 miles east on SR 40. Turn left (north) on CR 11 and go 8 miles. Look for signs to Hopkins Prairie. Turn right (east) on FR 86. Follow the dirt road for 2 miles. Campground and trailhead will be on the left (north) side of the road.

Traveling east on FR 86 is one of the most pleasing drives in the Ocala National Forest. The first view of Hopkins Prairie will be on the left, and it's a humdinger. You'll pass a parking lot for an old forgotten boat ramp, testimony to better days when the water levels were much higher. In another 200 yards is a left turn that will take you to the campground and trailhead. Cruise the loop at the campground. Most of the primitive sites are private and come with a superb view of a wet North Florida prairie.

At the trailhead, hike north on the Florida National Scenic Trail. The hike is gentle and easy as you skirt the edge of Hopkins Prairie. Some sections may be sandy. Hike in 1 to 3 miles and come back after sunset. Many small ponds with white sand beaches line the trail. Several delightful spots beg for you to stop and relax.

Please trust me when I tell you not to drink any surface water. Other trail guides might rave about the numerous water sources along the Florida Trail. If the water is not from a pump at one of the several campgrounds along the way, I wouldn't drink it. Yes, you can boil, filter or use pills, but it's still standing water—a gamble. Your source may be clear and spring-fed, but when I look at it all I see is the stuff doctors give you the night before a colonoscopy. Odds are you will be okay, or you could suffer from days of severe intestinal activity followed by a trip to the doctor. To me, it's not worth it. Always pack your water.

Scrub forest, sand pine and oak hammocks ring the massive wet prairies. At 0.5 miles, look back at Hopkins Prairie campground. It will appear as an oak oasis in the center of a misty grassland. On the shorelines, sandhill cranes gather for parties, kingfishers buzz above the ponds, and bald eagle and osprey hold court in the skies.

Much of the first mile is lined with blueberry bushes, a reminder that this is bear country. Also, along the palmettos near the water there could be rattlesnakes. You're in little or no danger, just be aware of your surroundings. On this very trail, I had a stare down with a four-foot eastern diamondback. He sat coiled in the middle of the trail and would neither move nor rattle. I backed up until I was out of sight and waited five minutes. When I walked back to the spot—presto!—the snake was gone. After one mile you'll be able to pick out several spots for a picnic. Many backpacking campsites also line the trail. The sky is wide open and drips with blue honey.

    Two friends accompanied me on my last hike at Hopkins Prairie. When we finished our hike we picked out a campsite with a gorgeous view and lit a campfire. As we watched the sun setting over the prairie, one of my friends sat in his chair and dug in the sand with a stick. We'll call him John. My other friend, a retired major in the USAF, watched him. We'll call him Rob. The tranquility of the scene had stifled our conversation and put us in a near hypnotic state.

    John found an old cigarette lighter in the sand. He brushed it off and flicked it several times. When it wouldn't light, he tossed it into the fire.

    I looked at him. "What'd you do that for?"
    "What?"
    Major Rob said, "That lighter could explode."
    John looked at us both. "No way."
    KAPOW!
    Sparks and bits from the fire landed in our laps.
    Major Rob frowned. "I thought you were an Eagle Scout, dumbass."

    This might be a good opportunity to mention the fact that many campers are closet pyromaniacs and arsonists. Sitting around a campfire is a grand and soothing experience, but the blaze needn't be a towering inferno. I've seen campers scorch the lower branches of trees with their bonfires. I've seen chairs and tents catch fire. When fires don't start easily, I've seen campers pour Coleman gas on the wood and have flames leap up to the can and burn their hands and arms.

    Please don't forget Smokey the Bear. Only you can prevent forest fires.

Hike # 12

Florida National Scenic Trail
Woody's Trail North

The sun, with all those planets revolving around it and dependent on it, can still ripen a bunch of grapes as if it had nothing else in the universe to do."

- Galileo Galilei

Directions – From Ocala, drive 5 miles east on SR 40. Turn left (north) on CR 314. Go 18 miles toward Salt Springs. The Florida Trail trailhead is on both sides of the road. The sign is small, so look carefully. If you pass CR 11 you've gone too far.

Be sure to lock your car. Many colorful characters living in the Ocala National Forest may recognize opportunity. Hike north on the Florida Trail for 1 to 3 miles. My suggestion is to go 1.5 miles and find a shady spot to relax among the stately longleaf pines.

I named this trail in honor of my beloved 95-pound Labrador who hiked and camped with me on this trail many times. Actually, I hiked and Woody galloped. Whenever I parked the truck, Woody would not even allow me to open the door. Instead, he pounced on my lap, all paws and tongue, and leaped out the car window. Then he would vanish down the trail. He did like to keep tabs on me, though, and would come back just to make sure I was still following. Then he was off again. I had to carry lots of water for him.

At 1.5 miles you'll be standing in the middle of Salt Springs Island. Forest islands are not surrounded by water in the traditional sense. They are islands of higher dry ground surrounded by lower flatwoods or sub-tropical swamps. They are usually packed with thick groves of towering longleaf or slash pines with a cover of knee-high wiregrass.

This section of Salt Springs Island is surreal and magical. Set up a chair and be mystified by the optical illusions created by the tiny lanes between thousands of trees standing as straight as arrows. The forest simulates a giant house-of-mirrors effect. Stand up and do a 360. Watch for a deer or fox peeking around a trunk. As the cool breeze kisses your face and ruffles your hair, listen for the red-tailed hawks screeching overhead. Many lanes between the trees will vanish when you blink, and reveal new ones. (John Muir once wrote, "Between every two pines is a doorway to a new world.") At sunset, the tree trunks and pine needles will glisten and reflect the colors of the sky while creating a surrealistic painting that spreads across your entire field of vision.

During one of my visits, two horseback riders meandered slowly through the yellow wiregrass. Woody's ears perked up.

"Don't worry," I said, sitting up in my chair. "He won't bother the horses."

It was a middle-aged couple. Both of them possessed a look of disbelief.

The man laughed and said, "We were intrigued by the image of a solitary man sitting in a chair in the middle of the woods."

"I'm just off the trail," I said, and pointed. "See the orange markers on those trees?"

"I don't like the Florida Trail," the woman said. "It doesn't allow horses."

"There are plenty of horse trails that don't allow hikers," I countered.

"Doesn't that make you mad?"

"No, it doesn't," I said. "We may have different agendas, but we both need wilderness and trails. If we stand together, we can save more forests."

She tilted her head. "I never thought about it like that."

A huge fog bank poured between the trees from the north. It was rapidly approaching our position.

"Now that's a surreal image," the man said. "Good luck." They turned their horses to the south and began to trot.

The first wisps of mist reached my chair. The heavier fog bank was still 70 yards away but rolling in quickly. A more haunting scene is difficult to imagine. I got a fire going and prepared to hunker down. Then I heard the loud clicks of hiking poles. I looked and saw my old friend the pole-hiker marching at a rapid pace from the north and barely keeping ahead of the fog. With each long stride, he quickly slung his poles and seemed to be in quite a rush to reach the highway.

"Hello, sport," I said.

He appeared relieved to see me, and treated Woody like a lost friend.

"Good boy, Woody," he puffed, nervously. "I'm glad to see you both."

"What's wrong?"

He looked north. "That fog bank is freaking me out," he said. "It came in fast and has been chasing me for thirty minutes. I started hearing noises."

"What kind of noises?"

"Heavy footsteps. Something was flanking me."

"Calm down, dude," I said. "You're starting to freak me out."

"It was either a bear or…"

"Or?"

"I don't know. A Bigfoot, or some other kind of demon stalker."

I burst out laughing. "There's nothing out here that can hurt you."

By this time we were encased in a crackling, dripping fog that blotted out most of the forest. I uncorked my wine.

"Hike out with me?" he asked.

"I just got my fire going. Sit down and have a cup of wine."

He shook his head vigorously. "I'm going to blow this pop stand."

"You're not going to abandon me to the demon stalker, are you?"

"At least you have Woody to protect you."

I smiled. "Woody would run like hell if he saw a ghost."

On your way back to Ocala, stop at the white church with a graveyard in Scrambletown. It's just off CR 314 on a small dirt road. Ask for directions at Bob's Country Store.

On November 20, 2011 a professional paranormal team reported several spooky occurrences, including the front door opening and slamming shut several times as they approached the church. They claimed there was no wind and no person or animal inside. While investigating the cemetery, two researchers reported feeling little fingers pinching their legs near a tombstone marked simply Baby. The entire team briefly saw a distorted image of a woman on the back porch of the church. Supposedly, they captured the image on film.

I've been there several times and had no paranormal experiences. But maybe you'll be luckier. Maybe Baby will take a liking to you.

Hike # 13

Longleaf Flatwoods Preserve Longleaf Trail

" *'Why did you look at the sunset?'*
Philip answered with his mouth full:
'Because I was happy.'"
                              - W. Somerset Maugham

Directions – From Ocala, drive 11 miles north on US 441-301. Merge to the right on US 301. Go 12 miles north to Island Grove. Turn left (west) on CR 325 and pass through Cross Creek. Go 6 miles northwest. Look for trailhead on the left (west) side of road.

Wedged between Orange Lake, Paynes Prairie and Lake Lochloosa is a splendid 2,856-acre parcel called Longleaf Flatwoods Preserve. The acreage is part of the Lochloosa Wildlife Florida Forever and Alachua County Forever projects. It is one piece of a large puzzle that connects a dozen other parcels in Alachua County totaling over 70,000 acres. The preserve is a stunning example of a longleaf pine-dominated flatwoods. Much of the property is in the process of restoration from extensive logging and southern pine beetle infestation. Other sections, however, contain many 100-year-old longleaf pines.

At one time the tranquil longleaf pine blanketed 92 million acres across the southeastern United States. It was a valuable resource for early settlers because the lumber was strong enough for railroad tracks, ships and buildings. Unfortunately, foresters replaced the longleaf with fast-growing slash and loblolly pines. By the 20th century, longleaf pine forests had been reduced to less than 3% of their historic range. The tree had become endangered.

So what?

Longleaf pine forests provide crucial habitat for more than 30 federally protected species and for hundreds of plants found nowhere else on earth. These forests supply clean water by absorbing rainfall, refilling ground water aquifers, filtering storm water runoff and maintaining watershed stability. The tree is also high quality timber. Restoration of longleaf pine forests has become a major conservation priority in recent years. All this and we haven't spoken a word about their beauty. Hiking in a mature longleaf pine forest will startle your perception and blow your mind with what I have called their house-of-mirrors effect. It is indescribably delicious.

From the usually empty parking lot, pass through the gate and walk to the trailhead kiosk for a trail map. The outer loop of the yellow and red trails is 4.4 miles, or you can customize your hike for a longer or shorter distance by utilizing the several inner loops. To start your hike, turn left on the white trail. The trail is well marked and comfortably wide.

Almost immediately you'll be hiking through the first section of a tall and mature longleaf pine grove with lots of shade. On the fringes of the trail are stands of rusty lyonia, with their crooked arms reaching out as if to grab someone. (The rusty lyonia is the exact type of tree the Grimm Brothers call to mind with their spooky descriptions of forests in stories like "Hansel and Gretel" and "Little Red Riding Hood.")

Careful, parts of the trail may be seasonably wet. And it's always a good idea to watch for snakes—this is North Florida.

Kiosk signage claims the reserve has white-tailed deer, wild turkey and gopher tortoise. I didn't see any, but I did see and hear several red-tailed hawks screeching from the treetops.

The kiosk info also says that one day bear might find a corridor to the preserve. This is incorrect. A large fresh pile of bear scat told me they've already arrived.

It was hunting season, and I could hear gunshots coming from the Lochloosa Wildlife Management Area, so maybe the poor bear was running for his life. Although bear hunting is still illegal in the state of Florida, there are hunters who will shoot them given the opportunity. If caught, they can always claim the bear charged them. Filthy scoundrels! (See p. 24.)

At the second fork, take the yellow trail to the left. Actually, first take a break. This is an excellent spot to relax. The hooded pitcher plant grows nearby. It's on the state's list of endangered and threatened plants, so tread gently. Also, many exceptionally tall longleaf and slash pine are in the area. Large oaks fill a small expanse to the right.

Continue on the yellow trail. The further you go the more spectacular are the oaks. Skip the trail to the dried-up Palatka Pond; it's quite unremarkable.

At the red trail fork, go in either direction. You'll be hiking among newly planted longleaf pines, signifying an attempt at restoration. Most are 15 to 20 feet tall. The open expanses are former pastureland, but if frogs are croaking, it's marshland. Along the old fence, wooly paw paw leave a trace of sweet fragrance in the air. Milkweed amongst the wiregrass may have a pale pink flower.

At the primitive campsite, live oaks, blackjacks and smaller turkey oaks surround the fire pit. It's a decent spot for an overnight stay. As you wind your way back to the trailhead, you'll return to the much larger groves of longleaf pines.

Sidenote: Between the Longleaf Flatwoods Preserve and the River Styx is Lochloosa Wildlife Management Area. Deep within the management area is a place called Burnt Island. Marjorie Kinnan Rawlins described Burnt Island in her novel *Cross Creek*:

"There was believed to be the grandfather of all rattlesnakes living there. Only glimpses had been had of him, but several reported to have seen his shed skin, and all agreed that it was nine-feet long.... There were wild boars on Burnt Island, savage, long-tusked and

dangerous. The place was also a hideout for criminals who preferred the great rattler and boars to the arm of the law."

Yipes! Enter if you dare.

Hike # 14

Florida National Scenic Trail
Hidden Pond

"We know that God is everywhere: but certainly we feel his presence most when his works are on the grandest scale spread before us."
- Charlotte Bronte

Directions – From Ocala, drive east on SR 40 for 26 miles to the entrance to Juniper Springs Recreation Area. Turn left (north) and pay the $5.50 entrance fee. Trailhead is on the road to the pay booth.

After parking your car at the recreation parking lot, walk back down the entrance road and watch for the Florida National Scenic Trail signs. Turn right to begin your hike. Don't be angry about paying the fee. No parking is allowed on SR 40 within 0.25 miles of the entrance. Plus, your car will be safe, and there's a surprise waiting for you after your hike.

At 11 miles roundtrip, Hidden Pond is the longest hike in this book, but it is a dandy. If you don't feel up to hiking the entire distance, turn around at any time you please. You'll find plenty of vistas and wet expanses after the first mile, excellent spots for a picnic. At 0.5 miles is the Juniper Prairie Wilderness sign. It's safe to hike in the wilderness area year-round because hunting is not allowed. You may, however, hear gunshots during the season.

Hidden Pond is the most popular and revered backpacking site in the Ocala National Forest. Unlike most prairie ponds, Hidden Pond is a crystal clear spring-fed pond with some depth and is great for swimming. It's also a prime destination for backpackers throughout the state, with dozens of gorgeous campsites ringing the pond and neighboring prairies. Everyone who hikes in North Florida must visit Hidden Pond at least once.

At 2.5 miles is a scenic prairie on both sides of the trail. Look to the right for the Sabal palms on the edge of Juniper Run, a crackerjack seven-mile canoe/kayak trail that is legendary for its remoteness and beauty. I would advise not to attempt a bushwhack at this point unless you're not adverse to ticks, chiggers and rattlesnakes. After passing out of the prairie, you'll discover several scenic oak hammocks, great places to rest or picnic. The trail crosses Whispering Creek and you might have to slog through some mud, but most of the remaining hike is through a thick sand pine forest with occasional prairie views. Look for otters splashing near the shorelines. Juniper Prairie Wilderness is also home to a large contingent of coyotes.

As you near Hidden Pond you'll pass through a forest of blackened skeletons within a new growth of palmettos. On March 10, 2009, following an extended drought, an escaped campfire south of Hidden Pond scorched 2,600 acres of sand pine. What is it with people and fire? Why do so many seemingly normal people turn into raving pyromaniacs in the woods? What is the fascination with bonfires? The so-called Indian fire is a small blaze that campers can huddle around, rather than having to pull their chairs back from a raging inferno. Oops, I apologize. I guess we've already covered this topic.

Just before the slight rise leading to Hidden Pond, an unmarked side trail on the right invites you to hike to Juniper Run. This trail is doable. Take your bearings, check your compass and add another hour to your hike. The trail roughly follows a trickle of mud called Whiskey Creek, a name that tickles the imagination.

The first view of Hidden Pond is stunning. Be sure to turn left just past the pond and hike over the rise for an unparalleled view of several spectacular wet prairies. This is my favorite spot to camp. The prairies usually ensure a steady cooling breeze with hints of pine and swamp water.

On my most recent backpacking trip to Hidden Pond, two buddies accompanied me. We'll call them Tom and Todd. In the morning, I was inside my tent rolling up my sleeping bag when I heard Todd say, "What the heck is this coming down the trail?" Then I heard a loud, high-pitched voice say, "Hi, I'm Harold."

When Harold asked for directions, Tom yelled, "Hey GK, get out here. This guy needs help." As I unzipped my tent flap, I could hear Todd telling Harold that I was the expert on trails in the Ocala National Forest.

I found Tom and Todd sitting next to a morning fire with their hats pulled over their eyes. A pint-sized skinny dude stood next to them wearing a bandana and hiking boots…and nothing else. Harold was nude.

"Hi GK," he said. "Do you know how to get to the Long Cemetery?"

I looked scornfully at Tom and Todd, who both shrugged, and back to Harold.

"Sure," I said. "Go back to the Florida Trail and hike north for three miles. You'll come to a signpost and a trail on the right. Follow that trail for one mile and the Long Cemetery will be on your right."

"Wow," Tom said after Harold left. "That took guts."

"Why do you say that?"

"This little guy named Harold walks into our camp naked. He doesn't know what kind of guys we are. We could've helped him, ignored him or conked him on the head and buried him out here."

"We didn't know what kind of guy he was either," Todd said. "He could've been a serial killer."

I shook my head. "I'm pretty sure Harold wasn't carrying any hidden weapons."

You may become a bit weary on the 5.5 return hike to your car. I understand and sympathize. That's why I saved the surprise for last. Change into your swimsuit and enjoy a refreshing plunge into Juniper

Springs. Members of Franklin Roosevelt's Civilian Conservation Corps built the walkways and old-fashioned water wheel in the 1930s. A plaque nearby relates their entire fascinating story.

Hike # 15

Alexander Springs Recreation Area Timucuan Trail

"Another glorious day, the air as delicious to the lungs as nectar to the tongue."
- John Muir

Directions – From Astor drive west on SR 40 for 2 miles. Turn left (south) on CR 445. Go 6 miles south and look for signs to the recreation area on the right (west) side of the road.

Alexander Springs is one of Florida's twenty-seven first magnitude springs. It is the best swimming hole in North Florida. The bewitching turquoise waters are extraordinarily clear and 35 feet down is a fine sandy bottom. The spring has easy access for swimmers, snorkelers and scuba divers. The run is great for canoes and kayaks. There are many documented stories about how Alexander Springs amazed Spanish and later English explorers.

One thousand years ago a prehistoric Timucuan culture thrived on the banks of the springs, for obvious reasons—water, fish and game. In the Timucuan culture the springs took on religious significance. The springs and surrounding area contributed greatly to survival. "Live as one" was the Timucuan model.

The 1.2-mile Timucuan Trail seems longer because of the many intriguing distractions. It took me over two hours to hike the trail. I must have made twenty stops. I did the hike on November 6, 2014 and was still a bit sweaty at the end, so I plunged into the gin colored waters of the springs. It was invigorating.

Enter the trail and turn left on the boardwalk to begin your loop. Prepare yourself for a wealth of stately Sabal palm groves. Also known as cabbage palm, the Sabal palm is Florida's, as well as South Carolina's, state tree. You'll also encounter cypress, oaks, maple, sweetgum and loblolly pines. As you step over a small spring-fed creek that empties into Alexander Run, notice the large clusters of saw palmettos. Native Americans used the plant for centuries as food and medicine. Modern herbalists cherish the berries for treating an enlarged prostate and as an aphrodisiac. Be aware, rattlesnakes have been known to nap under the fronds of saw palmettos. The forest also contains Atlantic white cedar, one of the strongest and most durable woods. The Timucuan used this tree to make their canoes.

Eventually you'll reach the first of two short spur trails on boardwalks that lead to observation decks on the river, or run. The first deck has a view of the swimming and canoe rental areas on the other side. The second deck has only river and wilderness as its view. Be prepared to spend some quality time on the second deck. Look for osprey, heron, wood stork and bald eagle. After leaving the second deck, turn left off the boardwalk and hike on the small dirt path. You will enter a thick forest of slash and loblolly pines, ancient cypress, palms and sweetgum. Also, the aroma of silk bay fills the air.

Mosquitoes can be fierce at any time of the year. Be sure to spray any exposed skin. Include cuffs and socks to guard against ticks and chiggers.

Continue on the dirt trail and you'll experience "The Real Florida" wilderness. Expect deer and raccoon to cross your path. Listen for the pileated woodpecker. No, they don't laugh like Woody. They have a variety of calls. You might hear a fairly high-pitched series of wuk, wok and wah. But the best way to spot a pileated woodpecker is to listen for loud hammering and follow it to its source.

Pause and rejuvenate your soul in a forest that makes you feel like you're living in prehistoric times. Note the swaying Spanish moss and wild edible grapes that grow on the fringes of the forest. This segment of the trail earns a double wow!

In the 1960s, two *Lassie* episodes were filmed near Alexander Springs. Handlers had trouble keeping the gorgeous collie from leaping into the water. Every time she went for a dip, production had to be halted in order to dry and brush out her coat. Once, her highness of acting dogs vanished for nearly thirty minutes causing a minor havoc among the crew. Supposedly, she emerged from the Timucuan Trail, tongue dragging and tail wagging.

Hike # 16

Billies Bay Wilderness

*"The wild places are where we began.
When they end, so do we."*
- David Brower

Directions – From Ocala, drive 32 miles east on SR 40. Turn right (south) on CR 445. Drive 6 miles south. Just past the entrance to Alexander Springs Recreation Area, look for a small Billies Bay Wilderness sign on the right (west) side of the road. FRS 538-2 is the first dirt road on the right.

I have never recommended a hike on an actual dirt road, but FRS 538-2 is just too awesome to pass up. It's a tiny single lane track that is quiet, isolated, beautiful, and it skirts the edge of the fabulous Billies Bay Wilderness. It travels about 5.5 miles from CR 445 to SR 19. Hike as far as you like and turn around. I promise you'll never tire of the views.

Warning: stay out of this area during hunting season.

Billies Bay Wilderness protects the headwaters of Alexander Springs and helps to keep its water pristine. The wilderness area is nearly inaccessible, although experienced bushwhackers will be able to make decent headway. I pushed in about 0.3 miles, and it was wild and scenic. I guarantee you won't see another human off the road. I explored the area for two consecutive days and saw one Jeep. Getting lost was never my concern, but unfortunately ticks are in abundance.

As you hike FR 538-2, a thick island of slash and loblolly pines is on your left, and the bay, with its pine, palm and cypress, to the right. Several kinds of oak, red maple and blackjacks are scattered throughout. Occasionally a nice expanse opens up with views. Old timers refer to swamps as bays, and Billies Bay is a prime example of a pristine North Florida swamp. Within the 3,092-acre tract, sunlight has a difficult time filtering to the ground. Thick palmettos and gallberry deter bushwhacking, but don't get discouraged. I discovered many avenues into the bay.

Legend has it that Seminole warrior Billie Bowlegs used the bay as a hideout during the Second Seminole Indian War (1835-1842). After the treacherous capture of Osceola under a white flag of truce, and the death of Micanopy, Bowlegs and his 200 warriors became the most prominent Seminole fighters. They survived until the hostilities ended on August 14, 1842.

Instead of following most of the Seminole to Oklahoma, Bowlegs and his band returned to Florida and lived in peace near the Big Cypress Swamp in Southwest Florida until 1855. At that time, a group of Army engineers and surveyors invaded his territory and chopped down his prize banana grove while constructing a fort. Some historians view these actions as an intentional provocation to force Bowlegs to fight and give settlers an excuse to kill or remove the last Seminoles from Florida. It worked. Bowlegs led his warriors in sporadic raids in what became known as the Third Seminole Indian War (1855-1858).

At first the Army couldn't catch or find the Seminole. Then, Colonel Gustavo Loomis came up with a clever new strategy of sending small, heavily-armed squads of Marines into the swamps aboard Alligator Boats, thirty-foot flatbeds that could skim shallow water and accommodate sixteen Marines. The strategy was highly successful. Marines surprised Seminole encampments and made quick work of the bands. In 1858, Loomis declared the war over. Bowlegs finally moved to Oklahoma and became a successful farmer. Many other Seminole, however, were never contacted or found, and remained in Florida. This Florida tribe of Seminole never surrendered to the United States. They declared neutrality in the Civil War and war on Nazi Germany and Japan during World War II.

The Billies Bay/Alexander Springs area has been the scene of many bizarre and disturbing incidents, including UFO sightings, disappearances and numerous sightings of the skunk ape, forest-speak for Bigfoot. If you hike FRS 538-2 or bushwhack Billies Bay, you may feel like you've disappeared. You will also be amidst the most desolate and seductive tracts in the Ocala National Forest.

Hike # 17

Florida National Scenic Trail
Farles Prairie

"Like music and art, love of nature is a common language that can transcend political and social boundaries."
- Jimmy Carter

Directions – From Ocala, drive 28 miles east on SR 40. Turn right (south) on SR 19 and go 6 miles. Turn right (west) on NFS 95 and drive 4 miles to Farles Prairie. Trailhead is on the right side of the road just past the picnic area.

If reports are true about the Florida Trail being moved to the east side of Farles Prairie, this could be another one of our secret hikes. The old trail on the west side should have far fewer, if any, hikers. In fact, the trail might become a "forgotten" section of the Florida Trail by everyone except us. On my most recent trip to Farles Prairie I couldn't locate the new trail, but it's probably still in development. Our trail on the west side of the prairie will obviously bear the orange blazes on the trees and should be no problem to follow.

Our trail is a 2.4 miles roundtrip that might require a small amount of easy bushwhacking to reach my secret spot, a circle of grass surrounded by tall slash and sand pine. To the north of the spot is a thick grove of sand pine, and to the south is a sweet view of a large pond. I've backpacked to the secret spot three times and never once run into other hikers. Tiny trails along the pond's shoreline, however, indicate that fishermen visit the area.

    Park your car on NFS 95 just west of the picnic area. Walk west and look for the trail and orange markers. (I'm assuming the Florida Trail signs will be removed.) Even without the signs, the trail should not be difficult to find. Hike north. The trail is slightly rolling, an oddity in North Florida. You will be immediately sucked into the middle of an ancient scrub forest, consisting of large stands of sand pine and towering slash pine. Blackjacks, myrtle and turkey oaks also inhabit the area. Lichen clings to the tree trunks, while Spanish moss sways with the breeze. Scrub jays call out to one another. The Florida scrub jay—sightings highly prized by birders—is the only species of bird endemic to Florida. It has been present in Florida as a distinct species for at least two million years.

    All animals indigenous to the Ocala National Forest might be spotted in this area. That means bear, deer, fox, bobcat and wild boar. In the wet areas, look for alligator. Step carefully around the wet stuff;

moccasin, aka cottonmouth, blends in with the weeds. Osprey nests are visible in trees surrounding the pond.

As you hike, notice the Florida rosemary growing out of the mossy understory. Points on the left will open up to large expanses, some with small ponds. One expanse in particular has been nicknamed "nightmare forest" because of its charred, spindly tree trunks, reportedly the victims of an errant bomb. Yes, I said bomb. To the west of the trail is a U. S. Naval Bombing Range. Navy jets fly down from all over the Southeast to dump their ordinance during practice runs. I've occasionally heard the booms, but I've never heard of an errant bomb, especially a bomb that could potentially kill people. Nevertheless the "nightmare forest" is charred. Plus, the place has some history. In 1942, Jimmy Doolittle and his squadron made several bombing runs over the range in preparation for their famous raid over Tokyo on April 18, 1942. Franklin Roosevelt was so adamant about initiating a quick and decisive response to the sneak-attack on Pearl Harbor, that when military advisors said a mission at that time was impossible, FDR supposedly stood up and said, "Don't tell me impossible."

At 1.2 miles, keep your eyes peeled for the pond on the right side of the trail. You'll see it first through a grove of slash pines. Once north of the pond, choose an open area and bushwhack east. Just north of the pond, you should be able to locate the pines that encircle the secret spot. It's a very hidden and scenic place to wile away the hours in adult activities.

Sidenote: Does a witches coven practice their craft near Farles Prairie? I've heard the rumors and questioned over twenty people in the know about the possibility of a witches coven around Farles Prairie. Most of the people responded with something like, "I don't doubt it," or "My cousin heard weird chanting," or "My niece saw a group of people wearing black hoods." On a solo backpack to the secret spot, I heard drums and tambourines for most of the night just north of my tent. In the morning I was determined to bushwhack north and discover the source of the all the hubbub. After hiking for twenty minutes I found stick figures hanging in the trees just like in the movie *The Blair Witch Project*. Finally, I came across an encampment of tents. It was quiet and no one seemed to be moving about. As I walked slowly, more tents came into view. A man wearing a black hoodie stood next to a tent and waved to me. I waved back.

"Hey brother," he yelled. "You got an extra doobie?"

Doobie? A witch wanted a doobie??

"Sorry dude," I yelled back. "I'm all out."

It turned out I had stumbled across an encampment of Rainbow People. They had been beating the drums and tambourines all night in a celebration. The Rainbow Family is a loosely affiliated group of individuals committed to the principles of non-violence, egalitarianism and peace on Earth. They organize assembly events throughout the nation called "gatherings." The gatherings take place at different times of the year in national forests in Montana, California, Colorado, North Carolina and Florida, and usually embody a post-hippie utopian style culture. At times they create problems with local merchants and law enforcement, but generally they cooperate and get along well with locals and the forest service.

Hallelujah! I may have single-handedly demolished the myth of a witches coven on Farles Prairie. I'll wager my friend's niece actually saw a group of Rainbow People wearing black hoodies.

Hike # 18

Clearwater Lake Trail and Florida National Scenic Trail from SR 42

"Love the world as you love yourself."
- Lao Tze

Directions – From the junction at SR 19 and SR 42 in Altoona, drive east on SR 42 for 6.4 miles. Entrance to Clearwater Lake Recreation Area is on the left (north) side of road. Turn left and take the first right to the parking lot.

My intent was to hike the St. Francis Loop off the St. Johns River in the extreme southeast corner of the Ocala National Forest. St. Francis is an 1800s ghost town on the river's shore. Unfortunately, I drove an hour and a half only to find the entrance to the St. Francis Loop roped off with a sign that read, "Trail Closed – Prescribed Burn." A pack of rangers stood next to the sign. I pulled up and the conversation went something like this:

"Hey," I said. "I don't see any smoke yet."

"Yes, sir. We're doing the prescribed burn tomorrow."

"What are you doing today?"

"Setting up the perimeter and logistics."

"Great. Can I do the hike?"

"No, sir."

"Why not?"

"I told you. We're doing a prescribed burn."

"But that's tomorrow."

"Right."

"Exactly."

He looked at his buddies and then back at me. "Sir, you need to move your vehicle. It's blocking our entry."

It's funny how forest officials used to call prescribed burns controlled burns. But often controlled burns became uncontrolled burns—"light 'em and fight 'em" being the unofficial Forest Service motto—so they changed the terminology. The art of forestry.

I drove to Clearwater Lake Recreation Area to hike the 1.3 miles Clearwater Lake Trail. Do not pay the entrance fee. Normally I support the forest service, but a $4.50 per person fee is a bit exorbitant for a 1.3 miles hike. Park in the first lot on the right. It's designated for Florida Trail hikers and is free. Walk fifty yards north on the paved road and drop into the loop on a small spur trail.

Signs at the trailhead warn about break-ins and vandalism to cars. Take your wallet with you and put anything else of value in the trunk. Cars left at trailheads can fall victim to thieves and pointy-headed vandals. The thieves know the owners are hiking, biking or backpacking. Your poor car is defenseless. Sadly, trailhead thievery is a universal problem. Cars parked at Appalachian and Pacific Crest trailheads are routinely looted. Crime rates stem from being near population centers. The Angeles National Forest near Los Angeles has been dubbed "the most dangerous vacation spot in America." Nice campgrounds and pretty forests attract their share of local locos. Be alert and sensible with your valuables.

Part of the Clearwater Lake Trail is an original segment of the Florida National Scenic Trail first blazed by Florida Trail Association founder Jim Kern and his volunteer work crew in 1966. The Association still clears and maintains the fabulous 1,300-mile trail, a crowning achievement dedicated to Florida hikers. Our hike is a gentle walk around a pristine North Florida spring-fed lake. Several benches dot the trail, offering picturesque views of the lake and surrounding forest.

Hike north. At 0.2 miles a short boardwalk takes you over a small wet area. Several longleaf pines have obvious V-notches on their trunks from turpentine tapping decades earlier. After 0.5 miles the trail reaches a bench with an exceptional view of the lake. Continue on through the scrub flatwoods. A bench at 1.0 mile marks the original starting point of the Florida Trail. Hike the final 0.3 miles and return to the parking lot.

Now you should be warmed up and ready to tackle another gorgeous section of the Florida National Scenic Trail. Start your hike by following the orange blazes north from the kiosk in the parking lot. Ignore a turnoff to the Paisley Woods Bicycle Trail and begin traversing a series of mounds covered by thick woods.

Just past the mounds you'll encounter several ATV trails. ATVs are not my favorite things in the woods. They're noisy and built to go off-road, which means many enthusiasts tear up the grasses and turn a pristine landscape into a sand box with tire tracks. However, if the forest service continues to develop off-road trails built specifically for ATVs, I'm all for it. ATVs can play on their designated trails and be welcomed into the alliance. Dirt bikes, too.

Rising out of a deep bowl, the trail pauses on a slight knoll with a horizon of rolling hills, then plunges into the heart of a classic longleaf pine island, perhaps the largest in the entire Ocala National Forest. Beautiful does not adequately describe this stretch of trail. Striking, spectacular and sublime are more like it. Colorful lupine and other wildflowers linger far into the winter. A slight haze blankets the tall wiregrass. The misty rolling terrain makes the scene appear mystical. This is the Florida Trail at its best.

After 2.7 miles you'll cross FR 538. Stand in the middle and look down both stretches of empty road. This is also known as the Paisley Woods Bicycle Trail, a great path for mountain bikes. I suggest you turn around at this point. If you continue, the island will slowly give way to a semi-tropical swamp.

Hike # 19

Emeralda Marsh Conservation Area

"I believe in God, only I spell it N-a-t-u-r-e."
                    - Frank Lloyd Wright

Directions – From Eustis, drive north on CR 452 for 8 miles. Turn left (west) on Emeralda Island Road. First parking lot is 5 miles on the left (east).

Emeralda Marsh Conservation Area is the crown jewel for bird watching in North Florida. Although the 7,089-acre preserve appears to be a secret outside of Lake County, local bird watchers and environmentalists rave about the large and diverse bird population. Also, the quick recovery of the marsh is a shining example of wetlands restoration.

In the 1940s the marshlands were drained and converted into cattle pastures and muck farms. Initial restoration began in 1974 when the area was designated a National Natural Landmark. Additional land purchases took place in 1991 and 1993. The property is part of a vast marsh system that historically surrounded Lake Griffin and the headwaters of the Ocklawaha River.

Without a doubt, the conservation area's star attraction is a 4.3-mile scenic drive on a small former dike that provides access to some of the finest bird observation sites in the state. John Stenbers, a district environmentalist, said, "I have talked to elderly enthusiasts and people in wheel chairs who are riding around and able to go birding. It [the scenic drive] is a great way to get people into the preserve that literally could not make a bike ride or walk over that distance." For the novice or advanced bird watcher, Emeralda Marsh presents unlimited opportunities.

    The scenic drive is open only Friday through Sunday, February to May, but a hiker can make the trip at any time, starting from the entrance or exit gates. There won't be any cars, and when the gates are locked most folks think the area is closed. Hike as far as you like. I guarantee a lovely trip with plenty of solitude.

    The birds of ACEHI, my acronym for anhinga, crane, egret, heron and ibis are hopping around everywhere. Storks, limpkin, pelican, osprey, hawk, bald eagle and nearly every type of duck can be sighted. The Ocklawaha Valley Audubon Society conducts a bird survey on the property every six months. Recent evidence is that the bird population is increasing, a healthy sign for the birds and for us.

    Other wildlife includes deer, fox, raccoon, bobcat, coyote, otter and various species of snake. The alligator population is one of the highest and most concentrated in North Florida.

    I thought we'd have a different kind of fun, a drive and hike, utilizing four short trails with trailheads within three miles of one another. Each trail offers a different example of life on the marsh. As you drive north on CR 452, be sure to skip the parking lot on the left side of the road. It is a parking lot to nowhere. I discovered no access trails near it. Also, be careful: many gates along Emeralda Island Road appear to be part of the conservation lands, but in reality are private properties. Locals who live out in a swamp have a tendency to be testy with trespassers.

At the first parking lot on the left side of Emeralda Island Road is our hike # 1. Even the parking lot is breathtaking. A couple of picnic tables would be superb. The trail, like all the other trails in the conservation area, is a former dike or road from the ranching and agriculture days. This trail immediately leads you for 0.25 miles through a spectacular oak and palm hammock. When it's breezy, the swaying palms with their rustling fronds, and the Spanish moss dancing in the air, create an almost dreamlike environment. At 0.3 miles, the marsh appears. Watch for blue herons and other wading birds. Oaks and palms can be seen in the far distance. This is an ideal spot to sit in your chair and enjoy luscious views of Emeralda Marsh. At 0.6 miles the trail dead-ends under a section of wet muck. Prepare to be muddy up to your knees if you push on. After your return to the parking lot you will have covered 1.2 miles.

Turn left out of the parking lot and our hike # 2 is 0.5 miles down the road. Look for the sign on the right that reads Public Fishing Pier and park on the opposite side of the road. Hike in 0.2 miles and look for the fishing pier/observation deck on the right. (It is slightly hidden by bushes.) Step onto the deck and let the birding begin. The view is a vast wetland choked with lily pads and stretching all the way to Lake Griffin. As I was there making notes for this book, a bald eagle streaked by at eye level, scanning the marsh for a meal. This is a spot to spend some quality time. The wind blowing off the marsh is cool and refreshing, smelling of aquatic plants with a hint of salt.

After returning to your car, again, turn left on Emeralda Island Road. The parking lot for hike # 3 is on the left after 1.1 miles. The trail starts off promising, amidst oaks and palms. Unfortunately, at 0.5 miles a huge yellow sign screams Warning: Beehives. I stopped and listened. Sure enough, there was a loud buzzing coming from a pile of white boxes. Bees!? Sounded like thousands of them. I was happy to hear them thriving, but dissuaded from continuing on the trail. I headed back to my truck. Total mileage is now 2.6, but you may want to skip hike # 3.

Hike # 4 is 0.6 miles farther south and the parking lot is on the right side of the road. This is the 4.3-mile Emeralda Marsh Interpretive Drive. It's Thursday and the gate is locked. There are no cars in the parking lot. Hmm. Nobody will be on the small dirt road if the gate is locked. Let's hike it.

As I slip on my daypack, two cars arrive, read the sign and drive off. Yes! At 0.3 miles a gate appears on the right. Snowy egrets play in a puddle. Wander about 200 yards down the trail to get a real sample of swamp life. At 0.5 miles the road makes a sweeping turn and the marsh opens up for some excellent birding. Total mileage for the four hikes is 3.6 miles.

Hike # 20

Lake Norris Conservation Area

"The butterfly counts not months but moments, and has enough time."
                              - Rabindranath Tagore

"Every thing in nature invites us constantly to be who we are."
                              - Gretel Ehrlich

Directions – From Weirsdale, drive east on SR 42 through Altoona. Turn right (south) on SR 439. At 6 miles turn left (east) on CR 44A. Drive 4.5 miles to Lake Norris Road. Turn left (north) and drive 2.5 miles to the conservation area's entrance on the left (west) side of the road.

The Lake Norris Conservation Area was purchased to protect the extensive hardwoods of Black Water Swamp, which lies on the western shore of the lake, and the shoreline of Black Water Creek, a major tributary to the Wekiva River. Lake Norris is a spectacular dark water lake that supports an impressive number of ospreys. Staff at the Boy Scout Camp located on the northern shore of the lake has reported counting more than 100 active nests in the cypress trees that ring the lake. The upland portion of Lake Norris Conservation Area consists of open improved pasture and striking pine islands. The area is a habitat for many birds and animals dependent on a wetland environment. The property also expands the corridor for the Florida black bear.

Lake Norris is part of a chain of lakes that environmentalists have targeted for clean up and preservation. Other lakes include Apopka, Harris, Eustis and Yale. For decades, industrial farms have dumped fertilizers with phosphorous into the lakes. This feeds algae and strangles a lake of its oxygen. Pesticides add nitrates and other toxic chemicals to the mix. The Wekiva-Ocala Greenway Florida Forever Program supplied funds used to purchase the Lake Norris parcel.

In November 2014, Amendment One, an initiated constitutional amendment, was placed before Florida voters. It sought to put 33% of the excise tax on documents into a land acquisition trust fund. The fund would purchase, protect and improve essential environmental tracts, including the endangered Everglades. It required 60% to pass and received 74.96%. The amendment will raise hundreds of millions of dollars over the next decade. The impressive number of votes cast for Amendment One indicates the citizens of Florida are demanding protection for their environment. Don't let government dictate environmental laws; government caters mostly to corporations and the elite. Don't let developers or any type of business dictate environmental laws; they don't care about Florida, they only care about profits. You and I are the only ones who truly care about Florida, and we passed Amendment One. The rallying cry has been sounded.

At the trailhead parking lot, three sandhill cranes greeted me with their smiling red, black and white faces: Larry, Moe and Curly Joe. Not another soul in sight. Where is everybody? The conservation area contains 3,536 acres.

Our hike is a 4.2 miles round trip. As you close the gate and leave your vehicle behind, you'll step into a world of primal beauty. The first 0.5 miles has an open expanse on the left and a mixture of oaks and palms on the right. It's a wide path that is actually a hard packed coquina road, a remnant from the old ranching and mining days. At 0.5 miles the trail dips into a mysterious and primordial swamp with a small bridge over a stream that empties into Black Water Creek. Linger on the bridge and listen to the running water or chortles of wild turkey. (I hiked this trail in January 2015, and I'm happy to report that I was not attacked by bugs, even in the swampy areas.)

At 1.1 miles the expanse on the left switches from oak and palm to an island of longleaf pines. An old barn on the right marks the site of a primitive campground with picnic tables and a fire ring. Make a sharp right and walk past a stack of canoes to the observation area of Lake Norris. Sadly, the view is limited and unremarkable. If the day is chilly, build a small fire back at the camp. There is a fine view of oaks, palms and the pine island from the tables. It's a nice place to rest and enjoy refreshments.

Continue west on the white blazed trail. The road turns into a grassy dirt path. On the right is the impenetrable Black Water Swamp. Turn your attention to the enchanting pine island on the left where the sunsets would make Georgia O'Keefe turn green with envy. When the pine area turns into an open expanse with scattered palms, you'll have your first view of a pond initially built by the Eustis Sand Mine Company. Careful: two horsemen I encountered said they routinely see several 12-foot alligators boldly sunning themselves on the trail. I didn't see any…but it's a nice place to turn around.

I've already mentioned how much I like round trip hikes because the trail always appears different on the hike back. Perhaps the different angles create new perspectives. The pine island, now on the right, seems even more enchanting with the colors of sunset. Slip over the small fence and explore the island. Spread out a blanket or raingear and enjoy an adult beverage. Cool breezes soothe your face, and rustle the palm fronds and pine needles.

My second visit to the lake observation site was more rewarding. For some reason I found I liked it better this time. Lake Norris is an alluring example of a dark-water North Florida Lake. The sound of waves lapping the shoreline is calming and hypnotic. I patiently waited for a visit from the Creature from the

Black Lagoon. I certainly wouldn't stick my big toe in the black water. Maybe the boy scouts from across the lake could come over and build an observation deck for an Eagle Scout project.

The three sandhill cranes were waiting next to my truck. I gave each one a large piece of bread from my second sandwich. It's not good to feed wild animals, but I felt they'd earned it by guarding my truck.

Hike # 21

Guana River State Park

> *"Our father who art in nature, who has given the gift of of survival to the coyote, the common brown rat, the English sparrow, the house fly and the moth, must have great and overwhelmingly love for no goods and blots-on-the-town and bums, and Mack and the boys. Our father who art in nature."*
> — John Steinbeck

Directions – Guana River State Park is located between Jacksonville and Vilano Beach on A1A. Access to trail is at the west end of the Guana River fishing dam. Parking for beach access is at three locations on west side of A1A.

Don't let the large crowd of fishermen on the dam deter you. That's where they'll stay. Once on the trail, it's usually a pretty lonely trek. Be sure to save this hike for after mid-January, when hunting season is over. The hiking trail is a small dirt road used by hunters during the season. Outside of hunting season, motorized vehicles are not allowed.

At 6 miles roundtrip, the hike is one of our longest, but you'll enjoy it. The hike is almost entirely in the shade, and your destination is a fabulous observation tower that overlooks the park and Lake Ponte Vedra.

For three miles, the hike leads through a captivating forest filled with oak, scrub habitat and hardwood hammocks. Within the 800 acres, you'll skirt pine flatwoods and salt-inland marshes. The area is a birders delight, with over 240 species and a dozen or more viewing areas along the marsh. Deer, wild turkey, armadillos and wild boar roam the woods. Take it easy and relax often.

Once you reach the tower, plan to spend some quality time on top. A lover of natural beauty could spend hours up there. Across from the lake there are sand dunes and the Atlantic Ocean. Cool ocean breezes dry the sweat on your face and arms, and might even rock the tower slightly. The view may well convince you to make this hike part of an all-day excursion, including a visit to the beach and to St. Augustine, the oldest town in the United States.

When you're ready to come down, return to your car on the same trail.

Guana River State Park boasts three separate parking areas for the beach, each section as attractive as the next. Choose a section and cross A1A to a walk-over-the-dunes boardwalk. At the top of the boardwalk you can decide which direction to explore. The entire beach area, over six miles, is totally undeveloped. It's incredibly refreshing to walk on a Florida beach without the ubiquitous hotels and condos. With the exception of Cape Canaveral National Seashore, the Guana River beaches are the finest stretches of pristine sand on Florida's Atlantic coast. The sand dunes glisten with sea oats, sea grass and sea grapes.

When the water is too cold, my favorite activity is to hunt for sea glass. Guana River is an excellent area to find high-quality polished pieces. Yes, at times I feel like a dork wandering aimlessly with hat and sunglasses while staring at the sand and poking things with my toes. But when you find that perfect piece of sea glass, smooth to the touch and frosted by the surf, it's just as rewarding as picking out a precious gem among the rocks on a mountain. Fill a pocket, if you can. I've found fine examples of blue, green, brown and clear, but never the Holy Grail of sea glass, a red piece.

Guana River marks the approximate spot of Ponce De Leon's famous landing in April 1513. Although he is credited with discovering Florida, Feast of Flowers, he apparently was not the first European to visit. It is said that when De Leon landed, the local Indians cursed at him in Spanish. Evidence points to Spanish slave traders raiding the Bahamas and hiding out on the Florida coast. It's a good guess those slave traders exhibited little kindness to the natives.

After your beach time, drive south on A1A toward Vilano Beach and enjoy a fabulous dinner at Cap's or Aunt Kate's. Turn right at the signs and drive toward the water. Both restaurants are superb, with indoor and outdoor seating on the Intercoastal Waterway. Lastly, discover the historic town of St.

Augustine, settled in 1565, over forty years before Jamestown. You might want to spend the night at the St. Francis Inn, with its resident ghost on the third floor, or at least take an evening stroll with one of the several ghost tours.

Hike # 22

Fort King National Historic Landmark Springs Loop Trail

"This is the only treaty I will make with the whites."
- Osceola, as he plunged a knife into the Treaty of Fort Gibson

Directions – From the downtown square in Ocala, drive 2 miles east on Fort King Street. Just after crossing 36th Avenue, look for the signs on the left (north) side of the road.

    Fort King National Historic Landmark is a surprisingly unspoiled natural area with nearly three miles of trails throughout thirty-eight acres smack dab within the Ocala city limits and two miles from the town square. When you pull into the small parking lot, it's hard to imagine the seclusion of these short trails and the isolation you will feel hiking them.

    Much of the credit for the preservation of this historic and natural site must go to the McCall family, who served as concerned and capable stewards of this unique parcel for over forty years. The family sold the property to Marion County and the City of Ocala in 2001. Many local groups and individuals, most notably the late Ocala city manager Paul Nugent, fought for the purchase and National Landmark designation of the Fort King site. The development of Fort King is an outstanding example of what county and city governments, along with a vigilant and determined group of individuals can accomplish when running on all cylinders. The non-profit Fort King Heritage Association was formed to protect, preserve and develop the park with the help of the city of Ocala government.

Located at 3925 East Fort King Street, three blocks east of 36th Avenue and the municipal golf course, the new park has a visitor center, memorial obelisk, picnic tables, benches strategically located along the trails, with a fine collection of interpretive signs and an authentic flagpole fashioned from a giant pine tree. A U.S. flag with 26 stars, from the era of the Second Seminole Indian War (1835-1842), flies proudly at the site. The park is open daily from sunrise to sunset and admission is free.

The nearly three miles of trails are delightfully lush and loaded with natural beauty. Many of the trees, including oaks and loblolly pines, are well over one hundred years old. A short 0.5-mile trail skirts the perimeter of the fort with interpretive signs explaining the many historical events that have occurred at the site. The park also has a surprisingly large amount of wildlife. Fox, deer and coyote patrol the grounds, while hawks and owls screech from the treetops.

My favorite trail is a 1.2-mile loop through the oldest section of the forest. It passes a small stream and springs that served as the water supply for the fort. My favorite bench on this loop is next to the small stream. It's a very soothing and relaxing place, and your chances of being alone are excellent. (Future plans call for a small bridge over the stream that will lead to an observation deck overlooking the springs.) I like to sit on the bench and let my mind drift in the flow of all that has happened right here. During the Second Seminole Indian War, armed soldiers were necessary to guard the men hauling water. Seminole warriors fought an exacting guerilla-style war of attrition; attacks from the thick forests surrounding the fort could erupt at any time.

The historical significance of the heritage site is huge. Fort King played a major role in the Second Seminole Indian War and served as the foundation for the city of Ocala. Built in 1827 and named after Colonel William King, the commander of the 4th Infantry, its purpose was to protect the Seminole tribes from greedy American land speculators and settlers. But in 1832, after the signing of the Treaty of Fort Gibson, the soldiers were instead instructed to expel the Indians from Florida and move them to Oklahoma. Fort King is the place where an enraged Osceola leaped to his feet and plunged a knife into the Treaty of Fort Gibson, shouting, "This is the only treaty I will make with the whites." A crease in the document at the National Archives attests to the incident.

This is also the site where, in December of 1835, Osceola shot and killed Indian agent Wily Thompson, a former general and U.S. Congressman, who was outside the ramparts of Fort King on his afternoon walk. This initiated the Second Seminole Indian War, the longest and most expensive Indian war in United States history.

Nearly every major officer in the U.S. Army at the time of the war made a stop at Fort King, including future president Zachary Taylor and future Mexican-American War hero Winfield Scott. Read *Amidst a Storm of Bullets,* a diary of Lt. Henry Prince, to get a feel for the fear factor experienced by young soldiers sent on day and night patrols in the thick forests surrounding the fort during the hostilities.

In 1837, Osceola was treacherously captured under a flag of truce, and died shortly after at Fort Moultrie in South Carolina. Most Americans believed the military's action to be disgraceful and despicable.

In 1846 the fort was dismantled for its lumber and the county courthouse moved to the new town of Ocala. The Fort King Heritage Association plans to build a replica fort, patterned after an excellent sketch of the original drawn by Lt. John Sprague in 1837.

Following your hike, head west on Fort King Street for two miles to Ocala's downtown square. Have a glass of wine at The Corkscrew or Wine Experience, followed by dinner at Mark's, Harry's or Pi.

Hike # 23

Ross Prairie State Forest Holly Hammock Loop Trail

"Coyotes move within a landscape of attentiveness. I have seen their eyes in the creosote bushes and among mesquite trees. They have watched me. And all the times that I saw no eyes, that I went walking and never knew, there were still coyotes."
- Craig Childs

Directions – From Ocala, drive southwest on SR 200 for 10 miles. After crossing CR 484, drive 1.5 miles and look for the Ross Prairie Trailhead on the left (south) side of the road.

Ross Prairie State Forest is a 3,527-acre tract acquired in 1995 by the Conservation and Recreation Lands (CARL) Program. The property is a multi-faceted recreation area and an outstanding example of the environmental alliance system. Recreational opportunities include hiking, biking, bird watching, backpacking, horseback riding and hunting. The alliance system works well on the CBS hit series *Survivor*, and if outdoor recreationists want to "survive" and be a force in the environmental wars, they must align and stay aligned.

The Holly Hammock Loop Trail is a 2.5-mile trail of exceptional charm. It provides opportunities for nature study, bird watching, backpacking and hiking all within oak and holly hammocks, pine islands and depression marshes. Start your hike on a narrow footpath and you'll immediately be immersed in a dense, shady oak and holly hammock. Florida sun can be a killer, even if you're protected by hat, sunglasses and plenty of sunscreen. Shade makes a big difference, and Holly Hammock provides shade for most of this hike. The oaks are massive and the stands of American holly are the largest I've ever seen. Many of the bigger oaks contain lush gardens of resurrection fern in the crooks of their branches.

At 0.4 miles, and with a little elevation, the trail enters an inviting longleaf pine island amidst a sea of wiregrass. In winter, winged sumac turns crimson and the red blanket lichens on the holly trunks are so bright they look like trail blazes. Quickly you return to a dense forest.

At 0.6 miles is the first dry prairie, with dikes along the edges built by ranchers who once owned the land. This is an exquisite spot to see sandhill crane and blue heron, or an occasional bald eagle. The American bald eagle has made a remarkable recovery in North Florida, mostly because of banned pesticides and habitat protection. America's symbol is not as rare as it was in the 1970s. Plunge back into the cool and mysterious darkness of the scrub forest and dip your head under the crooked arms of several large oak trees, including one monster that sits nearly in the center of the trail.

A sign marks a spur trail to a fine primitive backpacking campsite at 0.9 miles. Follow the green blazes to a small open area with a picnic table, fire grill and several places to pitch a tent. Call 352-732-1201 for a permit. Once you're back on the main trail, the thick and massive oaks continue to impress. These North Florida trees, with their Spanish moss swaying in full glory, are definitely the highlight of the loop.

Just beyond the campsite spur you'll approach the largest section of Ross Prairie that touches the trail. It's wet too. You'll be greeted by a panorama of grassland dotted with small ponds and a distant tree line. Stroll along the prairie to savor the view, but be wary of snakes and alligators. In late January of 2015, I was lucky enough to see a full moon rising over the prairie in the late afternoon, an inspiring sight.

One last bit of elevation and you're back in the luscious longleaf pine island, and close to the end of the loop. Holly Hammock Loop Trail is one of the most enchanting and lonely trails in North Florida.

Culinary Sidenote: Before you begin your hike at Holly Hammock, cross the bridge on SR 200 over the Withlacoochee River and breakfast at Red's, a local diamond in the rough. Florida cracker good!

Hike # 24

Carney Island Conservation Area

"When you're sad, my little star, go out of doors. It's always better underneath the open sky."
                                  - Eva Ibpotson

Directions – From Belleview, drive east on SR 25. Turn right (south) on SE 115th Avenue and follow signs to the entrance station.

Carney Island Conservation Area is actually a peninsula on Lake Weir. At one time it was called Lemon Point. Marion County's Pennies for Parks purchased Carney Island in 1990.

Spanish missionaries visited the area of Lake Weir and Lemon Point in the early 1600s. European diseases wiped out the Timucuan Indians before the padres could convert them to Catholicism. Seminole tribes lived on the point and around the lake in the 1800s. In fact, the lake was named in honor of a Lieutenant Ware, who was killed in an early U.S Army skirmish with Seminole warriors on the banks of the lake. (Over time, Ware transmuted to Weir. Weird, huh?)

In 1875, Captain John L. Carney purchased the land and it became known as Carney Island. John and his brother E.L. Carney turned the point into a successful citrus grove. Minute Maid later purchased the land, and in 1960 Coca-Cola bought Minute Maid. In 1990, Coca-Cola agreed with Marion County to a purchase price of $1.8 million, well under the appraised value. However, the property was found to be polluted by leaks from underground tanks that had held fuel used to power irrigation pumps in the citrus grove. Cost of the cleanup was estimated at $200,000 to $400,000. Rather than get involved in bickering and lengthy negotiations, Coca-Cola and the Marion County Commission agreed to split the cost of the cleanup, and the deal was finalized. Due to the vision and persistence of two Marion County Commissioners, Parnell Townley and Norm Perry, Marion County now owns 750 acres of woods and spectacular lake frontage.

Carney Island has excellent boat ramps, a swimming beach, clean restrooms and a dynamite 3.5-mile loop trail that takes you to the end of Lemon Point. The peninsula is naturally air conditioned with gentle breezes off Lake Weir, Marion County's largest lake at 5,700 acres.

Start your hike next to the picnic area. After 0.3 miles you'll reach the beginning of the first segment, known as Fern Gully Loop. Plenty of well-placed benches line the trail and invite the hiker to take a break. Watch for the endangered fox squirrel with its shiny black and tan coat. The peninsula also has a fair amount of deer and coyote, and loads of butterflies in season. Look higher for ospreys, hawks and bald eagles in flight.

Fern Gully passes a nice wetland that is dense with, go figure, ferns. At. 0.4 miles, take a right on Quail Loop. This is the loveliest section of the trail, with mature pines and oak hammocks. Hike leisurely. At 0.7 miles the Fox Trot Loop leads to the only access to Lake Weir. Sit on a bench at Lemon Point and enjoy the sights and sounds of this alluring lake. Return to the trailhead by following the second section of each loop. After your hike, swing over to the Eaton Beach Sand Bar and Grill on the southern shore of Lake Weir for a scrumptious lunch or dinner.

Historical Sidenote: On January 16, 1935, F.B.I. agents surrounded a two-story house on the north shore of Lake Weir and demanded that the occupants come out with their hands up. Supposedly, a gunman had attracted attention by trying to kill a legendary gator named Gator Joe. The man had been firing from a dock with a Tommy gun.

Alarmed neighbors called Marion County sheriffs, who in turn called the F.B.I. in Jacksonville. Upon being ordered to surrender, Ma Barker and her son Fred answered with a blaze of fire from automatic weapons and initiated a spectacular two-hour gun battle with dozens of G-men and local law enforcement. Many locals appeared on the scene with picnic baskets to watch the shoot-out. No agents were killed, but both

Barkers were found dead inside the house with multiple gunshot wounds.

The house still stands today and current efforts are under way for Marion County to buy the property and turn it into a historical park. In January of each year the shootout is re-enacted by volunteers and members of the Marion County Sheriffs Department. This story begs to be made into a quality movie in the same league as *Public Enemies* with Johnny Depp playing John Dillinger, or the classic *Bonnie and Clyde* with Warren Beatty and Faye Dunaway in the title roles.

Hike # 25

Withlacoochee State Forest
Oxbow Bend and Johnson Pond Trails

"I think it pisses God off if you walk by the color purple in a field somewhere and don't notice it."
- Alice Walker

"Spring is Nature's way of saying, 'Let's party.'"
- Robin Williams

Directions – From Ocala, drive 12 miles southwest on SR 200. Cross the Withlacoochee River and turn right (north) on CR 39. Go 3 miles north. Johnson Pond trailhead will be on the left (west) and the Oxbow Bend Trail is 200 yards north on the right (east) side of the road.

Our final trail is a treat and a bargain—two trails in one, both located in Two Mile Prairie, a 2,896-acre tract in the wild and isolated Withlacoochee State Forest. The shorter trail takes you to an oxbow bend in the Withlacoochee River, and the longer to a fabulous wet prairie called Johnson Pond.

Hike the Oxbow Bend Trail first. At 0.7 miles it's the shorter hike. The trail is a pleasant loop that leads to two outstanding views of the wild and undeveloped Withlacoochee River. Four separate Eagle Scout projects that included trail work, benches, picnic tables and fire rings were completed before the opening of the trail. Thank you, Scouts!

In Marion County the Silver, Rainbow and Ocklawaha rivers get all the press, but the Withlacoochee is longer and equally striking. Like the Ocklawaha, the Withlacoochee was nearly destroyed by the amazingly stupid plan to construct the Cross Florida Barge Canal. Fortunately, before any real dredging occurred on the Withlacoochee, President Richard M. Nixon pulled the plug on the project in 1971.

The Withlacoochee River originates in the Green Swamp north of Tampa and flows northwest to Yankeetown and the Gulf of Mexico. There's an interesting story about the Green Swamp. In August 1974, a Taiwanese national suffering from severe homesickness became violent on board his ship in Tampa Bay harbor. He was subdued by eight crewmen and taken to a local hospital. Almost immediately he disappeared. For the next eight months strange stories persisted about a human-like monster roaming the Green Swamp. Residents in the area were jittery. In April 1975, deputy sheriffs got close enough to the monster, described as a green cave man, to fire warning shots. A string of burglaries motivated the deputies to look further into the matter. Local and national newspapers filled their front pages with stories about the "Wild Man of the Green Swamp." On May 17, 1975 a posse, tipped off by a reported campfire, descended on the swamp to apprehend the green monster. What they found instead was a small, terrified Chinese man living mostly off armadillos and garbage. The first deputy to grab the wild man got his arm bitten. "He's a strong little rascal," the deputy later said. "Of course, he was scared to death."

While on the 0.7-mile Oxbow Bend loop, you can push for a longer distance on a scant trail along the river, but I'd advise against it because of chiggers, ticks and lack of quality views. The best river view is on the main trail at the bend for which it is named. Bring mosquito spray, even in the winter; the little buggers can be tenacious. I'd also recommend a cold day for this trail.

On the loop, good-sized oak, loblolly pine and cypress provide excellent shade. At 0.4 miles is a picnic table and incredible view of the river on a large oxbow, or bend. Crawl out on an oak branch and relax above the moving water. The primitive campsite is 0.2 miles further and has another lovely view of the river. The camp is spartan, with no tables or benches, only a fire ring.

If you're planning to fish the river, please don't leave your bait containers along the riverbank. Believe it or not, they miraculously turn into litter!

Back at the Oxbow Trail parking lot, walk or drive 200 yards south to the Johnson Pond trailhead on the right side of CR 39. The Johnson Pond Trail is a 2.6-mile loop. It's my favorite of these two, that's why I saved it for last. As you hike into the upland forest, cool breezes dry your sweat and cool your face. Although the longleaf pines are pretty, the real stars of this trail are turkey oaks and live oaks. Their crooked branches intermingle and create Jackson Pollack-style designs.

At 1.8 miles is an observation deck overlooking Johnson Pond. On my first visit, in November 2014, there was hardly any water in the pond, but in March of 2015 the entire expanse was flooded with beautiful blue water that even spread under the deck. Wait for sunset and relish the view. With proper timing during the month you can see the sun setting on one side of the pond while the moon rises on the other. The entire experience is magnificent, especially if you can see both orbs reflecting in the pond.

Hike the final 0.75 miles back to your car with flashlights or headlamps. Warning: the Two Mile Prairie Tract is connected to the Goethe State Forest by a corridor known as Bigfoot Highway.

After your hike, return to SR 200 and cross the Withlacoochee River bridge. On the left is Stump-knockers Restaurant with their famous all-you-can-eat fried catfish dinner, no bones. Enjoy an adult beverage and have your picture taken aboard the 16-foot stuffed alligator next to the outdoor bar. Cheers!

Epilogue – We Have To Care

"The tree that moves some to tears of joy is in the eyes of others only a green thing that stands in the way."
- William Blake

As citizens of the United States of America, we must do everything in our power, and more, to protect and defend the American landscape. We have to do it, you and me, there is nobody else.

We have to care.

"I'm a patriot of the North American continent."
—Utah Phillips

Happy Trails

"He that plants trees loves others besides himself."
                                                 - Thomas Fuller

Happy trails to you, until we meet again.
Happy trails to you, keep smilin' until then.
Who cares about the clouds when we're together?
Just sing a song and bring the sunny weather.
Happy trails to you, till we meet again.

(from "Happy Trails" by Dale Evans Rogers)

There Is Another Sky

There is another sky,
Ever serene and fair,
And there is another sunshine,
Though it be darkness there;
Never mind faded forests,
Never mind silent fields –
Here is a little forest,
Whose leaf is ever green,
Where not a forest has been;
In its unfading flowers
I hear the bright hum:
Prithee, my brother,
Into my garden come.

Emily Dickinson

Recommended Reading

1. *Paradise Screwed: Selected Columns,* Carl Hiassen

2. *Cross Creek,* Marjorie Kinnan Rawlins

3. *The Beach,* Alex Garland

4. *The Animal Dialogues: Uncommon Encounters in the Wild,* Craig Childs

5. *Hiking North Florida and the Panhandle: A guide to 30 Great Walking and Hiking Adventures,* M. Timothy O'Keefe

6. *National Audubon Society Field Guide to Florida*

7. *Journal of Light: The Visual Diary of a Florida Nature Photographer,* John Moran

8. *The Wild Heart of Florida: Florida Writers on Florida's Wilderness,* edited by Jeff Ripple and Susan Cerulean

9. *Florida's Magnificent Water,* James Valentine and D. Bruce Means

10. *Hayduke Lives,* Edward Abbey

Acknowledgments

I wish to express my sincere and profound appreciation for the stunningly beautiful region known as North Florida.

Thank you to my special friends for support and encouragement: Todd Carstenn, Rob Burgess, Brenda Dilley, Gary Greenfield, Dr. Susan Pierce, Tom Dann, MaryAnn Wilkinson, James Lindsay, Richard Knapp, Georganne Alex, Mike Newman, Peggy Coe Lewerenz and Dr. David Willis.

A huge thanks to my editor, Dan Barth. You are a friend and an inspiration.

About the Author

Born and raised in Los Angeles, G. Kent now lives in the wilds of the Ocala National Forest in North Florida. He is the author of *Hiking in North Florida with William Bartram – Volume One* (Bandit Press, 2014), *Running with Razors and Soul: A Handbook for Competitive Runners* (Bandit Press, 2013), and two novels, *Grinners* (Bandit Press, 2014) and *Bandits on the Rim* (Tenacity Press, 2012).

For more information, contact kentib@earthlink.net.

Front cover photo of Holly Hammock Trail and back cover photo of G. Kent with William Bartram sign by Rob Burgess.

www.ingramcontent.com/pod-product-compliance
Lightning Source LLC
Chambersburg PA
CBHW071509040426
42444CB00008B/1566